OPPOSING VIEWPOINTS®

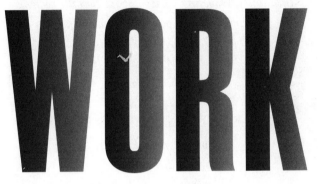

Other Books of Related Interest

OPPOSING VIEWPOINTS®

WORK

James Haley, *Book Editor*

Daniel Leone, *President*
Bonnie Szumski, *Publisher*
Scott Barbour, *Managing Editor*

OPPOSING
VIEWPOINTS®
SERIES

GREENHAVEN PRESS
SAN DIEGO, CALIFORNIA

GALE GROUP

THOMSON LEARNING

Detroit • New York • San Diego • San Francisco
Boston • New Haven, Conn. • Waterville, Maine
London • Munich

Cover photo: Photodisc

Library of Congress Cataloging-in-Publication Data

Work / James Haley, editor.
  p. cm. — (Opposing viewpoints series)
  Includes bibliographical references and index.
  ISBN 0-7377-0914-6 (pbk. : alk. paper) —
ISBN 0-7377-0915-4 (lib.)
  1. Working class—United States. 2. Labor unions—United
States. I. Haley, James, 1968– . II. Opposing viewpoints series
(Unnumbered).

HD8066 .W64 2002
331'.0973—dc21   2001040747
                                                        CIP

Copyright © 2002 by Greenhaven Press,
an imprint of The Gale Group
10911 Technology Place, San Diego, CA 92127

"Congress shall make
no law...abridging the
freedom of speech, or of
the press."

First Amendment to the U.S. Constitution

The basic foundation of our democracy is the First
Amendment guarantee of freedom of expression.
The Opposing Viewpoints Series is dedicated to the
concept of this basic freedom and the idea that it is
more important to practice it than to enshrine it.

Contents

**Chapter 3: What Role Should Labor Unions Play
in the Workplace?**

Chapter 4: How Should Equality in the Workplace Be Achieved?

Why Consider Opposing Viewpoints?

"The only way in which a human being can make some approach to knowing the whole of a subject is by hearing what can be said about it by persons of every variety of opinion and studying all modes in which it can be looked at by every character of mind. No wise man ever acquired his wisdom in any mode but this."

John Stuart Mill

In our media-intensive culture it is not difficult to find differing opinions. Thousands of newspapers and magazines and dozens of radio and television talk shows resound with differing points of view. The difficulty lies in deciding which opinion to agree with and which "experts" seem the most credible. The more inundated we become with differing opinions and claims, the more essential it is to hone critical reading and thinking skills to evaluate these ideas. Opposing Viewpoints books address this problem directly by presenting stimulating debates that can be used to enhance and teach these skills. The varied opinions contained in each book examine many different aspects of a single issue. While examining these conveniently edited opposing views, readers can develop critical thinking skills such as the ability to compare and contrast authors' credibility, facts, argumentation styles, use of persuasive techniques, and other stylistic tools. In short, the Opposing Viewpoints Series is an ideal way to attain the higher-level thinking and reading skills so essential in a culture of diverse and contradictory opinions.

In addition to providing a tool for critical thinking, Opposing Viewpoints books challenge readers to question their own strongly held opinions and assumptions. Most people form their opinions on the basis of upbringing, peer pressure, and personal, cultural, or professional bias. By reading carefully balanced opposing views, readers must directly confront new ideas as well as the opinions of those with whom they disagree. This is not to simplistically argue that everyone who reads opposing views will—or should— change his or her opinion. Instead, the series enhances readers' understanding of their own views by encouraging confrontation with opposing ideas. Careful examination of others' views can lead to the readers' understanding of the logical inconsistencies in their own opinions, perspective on why they hold an opinion, and the consideration of the possibility that their opinion requires further evaluation.

Evaluating Other Opinions

To ensure that this type of examination occurs, Opposing Viewpoints books present all types of opinions. Prominent spokespeople on different sides of each issue as well as well-known professionals from many disciplines challenge the reader. An additional goal of the series is to provide a forum for other, less known, or even unpopular viewpoints. The opinion of an ordinary person who has had to make the decision to cut off life support from a terminally ill relative, for example, may be just as valuable and provide just as much insight as a medical ethicist's professional opinion. The editors have two additional purposes in including these less known views. One, the editors encourage readers to respect others' opinions—even when not enhanced by professional credibility. It is only by reading or listening to and objectively evaluating others' ideas that one can determine whether they are worthy of consideration. Two, the inclusion of such viewpoints encourages the important critical thinking skill of objectively evaluating an author's credentials and bias. This evaluation will illuminate an author's reasons for taking a particular stance on an issue and will aid in readers' evaluation of the author's ideas.

It is our hope that these books will give readers a deeper understanding of the issues debated and an appreciation of the complexity of even seemingly simple issues when good and honest people disagree. This awareness is particularly important in a democratic society such as ours in which people enter into public debate to determine the common good. Those with whom one disagrees should not be regarded as enemies but rather as people whose views deserve careful examination and may shed light on one's own.

Thomas Jefferson once said that "difference of opinion leads to inquiry, and inquiry to truth." Jefferson, a broadly educated man, argued that "if a nation expects to be ignorant and free . . . it expects what never was and never will be." As individuals and as a nation, it is imperative that we consider the opinions of others and examine them with skill and discernment. The Opposing Viewpoints Series is intended to help readers achieve this goal.

David L. Bender and Bruno Leone,
Founders

Greenhaven Press anthologies primarily consist of previously published material taken from a variety of sources, including periodicals, books, scholarly journals, newspapers, government documents, and position papers from private and public organizations. These original sources are often edited for length and to ensure their accessibility for a young adult audience. The anthology editors also change the original titles of these works in order to clearly present the main thesis of each viewpoint and to explicitly indicate the opinion presented in the viewpoint. These alterations are made in consideration of both the reading and comprehension levels of a young adult audience. Every effort is made to ensure that Greenhaven Press accurately reflects the original intent of the authors included in this anthology.

Introduction

"The key to making work pay is encouraging employers to pay higher wages to people at the bottom."
    —Robert B. Reich, American Prospect, *June 19, 2000*

"Living wage laws offer us the temptation of legislating ourselves into prosperity. Only economic reality stands in the way."
    —*J.D. Tuccille, Free-Market.Net, October 25, 2000*

In 1991, the U.S. economy pulled out of a year-long recession and entered a period of sustained economic growth that was to become the longest boom in the nation's history by the start of the twenty-first century. Fueled by the technology revolution, the development of the Internet, and globalization, a flurry of entrepreneurial activity led to the rise of new businesses (albeit some short-lived) and the rapid expansion of existing ones. The economy favored the American worker with national unemployment rates at around 4 percent toward the end of the 1990s, their lowest since the late 1960s, drawing former welfare recipients, minorities, and the long-term unemployed into the workforce in unprecedented numbers. Demand for highly skilled workers also surged as the computer age gathered force, creating a new class of "overnight" millionaires.

Though many Americans have clearly benefited from this expansion, commentators are alarmed by what they contend is the widening gap between high-wage earners and the rest of the workforce. According to former secretary of labor Robert Reich, "[In 2000,] the richest 2.7 million Americans, comprising the top 1 percent, . . . [had] as many after-tax dollars to spend as the bottom 100 million put together, and . . . [they had] 40 percent of the nation's wealth." Unquestionably, the "new economy" has increased earnings for highly skilled workers—law firms, investment banks, and computer companies have spared no expense in attracting and holding on to employees in a tight labor market, where entry-level salaries have reached upwards of $120,000.

While the wages of skilled workers have increased, however, the wages of low-income workers have actually fallen over the past 30 years. The federal minimum wage, when adjusted for inflation, was worth nearly two dollars less in 1999 than in 1968, according to a study on low-wage earners by Jared Bernstein and John Schmitt of the Economic Policy Institute. Explain Bernstein and Schmitt, "Back in 1968, full-time work at the minimum wage put a . . . [one-parent family with two children] about $1300 (in 1999 dollars) above the poverty line. . . . [In 1999,] that same family would be $2700 below the line." As reported by the Bureau of Labor Statistics, 4.4 million out of the 130 million workers nationwide earned the minimum wage in 1999. Over 20 million Americans are considered low-wage workers, earning under $7.15 an hour, and many of them are parents supporting families.

In response to the stagnating wages of low-wage workers and the widening income gap between rich and poor Americans, unions, community groups, and religious organizations have begun promoting the idea of a "living wage," defined as the wage necessary for one earner to support a family of four above the poverty line of $17,000 a year. This wage works out to about $8.20 an hour for a forty hour workweek. The living wage idea is based on the belief that in a society that discourages dependency and where work is highly regarded, no one should work full-time and still struggle to keep a family out of poverty. In 1994, Baltimore was one of the first cities to enact a living-wage ordinance, establishing a government-mandated hourly wage of $7.70 for contractors and subcontractors doing business with the city. Since that time, numerous cities around the country have passed living wage ordinances, with hourly wages ranging from around $8 to $11. Advocates are also pushing for federal living wage legislation to replace the minimum wage on a national scale.

Living-wage proponents argue that the insufficient federal minimum wage is in part responsible for the large number of working poor in the United States. David Moberg, a senior fellow of the Nation Institute, a liberal research organization, argues that in paying low wages, businesses are in fact being subsidized by taxpayers, who must make up the difference in workers' low pay and lack of health insurance with medical care, food stamps, and tax credits. Contends Moberg, "Why should businesses be allowed to slough off these costs onto taxpayers? And if taxpayers are ultimately paying the wages of contract employees anyway, why not simply pay the employees a living wage directly?" Contrary to conventional economists who believe that raising the minimum wage reduces employment and hurts the poor, Moberg asserts that "employers compensate for higher wages by managing better, . . . saving on turnover and recruitment expenses, and gaining productivity from a more motivated work force."

Opponents contend that living wage laws are not the right approach to correcting the income gap between high-wage and low-wage workers. According to a report on the American workforce by the Hudson Institute, a conservative policy research organization, education is the key to better wages; the earnings of college-educated workers are substantially higher than those with only a high school diploma. In addition, fears that economic inequality is rising are based on "'static' snapshots of income distribution at a particular moment in time," according to the report. It is more realistic, in the opinion of the authors, to examine whether low-wage earners are increasing their earnings over time. Concludes the Hudson Institute, "Data from . . . [a] U.S. Treasury Department . . . study [finds that] 86 percent of those in the lowest income bracket in 1979 moved up to a higher bracket within nine years. Two-thirds of these Americans moved into the top three quintiles, and 15 percent of them moved all the way up into the top quintile of earners."

Critics further argue that under the artificially high wages proposed by living wage advocates, low-skilled workers will have a harder time finding work in the first place, let alone moving up the income ladder, as businesses shed workers they can no longer afford to keep on the payroll. W. Michael Cox, a senior vice president and economist at the Federal Reserve Bank in Dallas, and Richard Alm, a business reporter at the *Dallas Morning News*, assert, "If government dictum replaces market reality, jobs will be lost or never created. . . . What's worse, local governments' intervention in the free market sends an anti-business signal: Don't come here. Go elsewhere. And companies will do that, taking their jobs and tax payments with them." As the living wage movement expands to more cities, and threatens to move onto state and national levels, Cox and Alm foresee drastic consequences for America's economy, with slower business growth and higher rates of unemployment.

It remains to be seen whether living wage laws are the answer to raising the living standards of low-wage workers and slowing the divide between America's rich and poor, but the movement has quickly gained momentum and brought attention to those on the short end of an economic boom. What seems clear, however, is that in an economy shaken to the core by technology and the flexibility demanded by globalization, American workers of all income levels are facing a rapidly changing job market that requires a fleetfooted vigilance to navigate. The policies, conditions, and changes affecting America's workforce are debated and discussed in *Work: Opposing Viewpoints*, which contains the following chapters: How Should the U.S. Workforce Be Educated? Should the Government Intervene in the Job Market? What Role Should Labor Unions Play in the Workplace? How Should Equality in the Workplace Be Achieved? These chapters uncover the forces affecting the American workforce as the turn-of-the-century information and technology revolution continues its unstoppable march to the future.

CHAPTER 1

How Should the U.S. Workforce Be Educated?

Chapter Preface

The 1990s saw the emergence of an information-based service economy driven largely by rapid advances in technology. While the low unemployment rates experienced throughout much of the 1990s and into the twenty-first century attest to the strength of this transformation, many business leaders have expressed concern that the U.S. education system is failing to produce workers capable of performing in today's highly skilled, knowledge-intensive labor market.

Many educators and business leaders are convinced that one solution is to expand job training efforts, in particular the school-to-work programs for high school students, based loosely on Germany's dual education system. In Germany, students who do not plan to continue into higher education enroll in occupational apprenticeships while they attend school, leaving high school with marketable job skills. School-to-work programs in the United States are designed with similar intent, but have yet to achieve the scale of the German system. According to Arnold Offner, an executive with the Phoenix Contact corporation, "There is no quick and easy solution to the shortage of skills, but . . . the benefits [of apprenticeships] will far outweigh the investment in the most dynamic of resources within the U.S., its people."

Critics charge that school-to-work and job training programs underemphasize traditional academics and assert that without high academic standards the programs will not adequately prepare students for skilled employment. William G. Durden, director of the Institute for the Academic Advancement of Youth, argues that "school-to-work cannot evade the problems of the American classrooms from which it draws. And the learning needs of children must not be neglected as we fantasize about their competence as adults."

The education that Americans attain before entering the workforce is central to sustaining the country's economic success and high standard of living. How a well-prepared workforce can best be developed is debated and analyzed in the following chapter.

> *"There's evidence . . . that students involved in extensive school-to-work programs have achieved higher grades and have gone on to college in greater numbers than their classmates."*

The Education System Should Emphasize Work Skills

Pamela Emanoil

In the following viewpoint, Pamela Emanoil maintains that school-to-work programs have been effective in helping high school students choose and achieve career goals. These programs put students to work in part-time occupational apprenticeships, providing them with specific skills and helping them find a career path, according to the author. Emanoil describes a successful demonstration project that became the framework for the federal government's school-to-work program. Emanoil is a journalist and writer for the Media and Technology Services Department of Cornell University.

As you read, consider the following questions:

1. In the author's opinion, what problem among high school graduates are school-to-work programs intended to address?
2. What segment of the student population, in Emanoil's opinion, would benefit most from work-based learning?
3. In what ways did the Hamiltons modify the German style of apprenticeship, according to Emanoil?

Excerpted from "Working to Learn," by Pamela Emanoil, *Human Ecology*, vol. 29, no. 1 (Winter 2001), p. 18. Reprinted with permission.

For many teenagers, school is impractical and irrelevant. So they often become more engaged in dead-end, low-paying after-school jobs. Two researchers have initiated opportunities for youth to combine school and work in preparation for careers.

Lisa Wolf entered the apprenticeship program in 1993 when she was a junior in high school. She worked as a human resources clerk for Anitec, a Binghamton, N.Y., manufacturing facility, where she did filing and data entry. When she graduated from high school, she stayed on at Anitec for five years, gradually assuming more responsibility in its human resources department. . . .

What's more, Wolf continued her education during those years, receiving degrees from Broome County Community College and Binghamton University. In 1999 she began working for Mom's House, a day care program for parents continuing their education, as an assistant administrator.

By the time Lisa Wolf turned 21, she had worked for five years in a human resources office, filing reports, facilitating benefits, and maintaining a database. She also was close to receiving a college degree. "Not many 21-year-olds can say that," she says. "I had a wonderful opportunity."

Linking the Classroom with Work

That opportunity was an apprenticeship program that began as a four-year demonstration project in Broome County, New York, in 1990. It was initiated by Stephen Hamilton, professor of human development [at Cornell University], and Mary Agnes Hamilton, senior research associate, to adapt elements of European apprenticeships and to provide opportunities for youth to learn work.

"In the United States, the emphasis has been on classroom-based instruction," says Stephen Hamilton. "By senior year in high school, three-fourths or more of students are working after school, but they usually work in low-level jobs. They learn a few things, but what they learn can be learned in a matter of weeks. They go on working just to make money."

According to Hamilton, these working students get distracted from school. Their grades plummet, and they end up unprepared for the future, with few job skills.

The demonstration project in Broome County was designed to link work experiences and classroom experiences and to test approaches that could be used in a more comprehensive school-to-work system. In fact, the lessons learned from the demonstration project informed the Federal School-to-Work Opportunity Act, which was signed into law by [former] President Clinton in May 1994. The act provides funds to states and local communities to develop school-to-work programs that expose students to a broad variety of career options, starting with speakers and field trips in elementary school and moving to internships in high school. The object is to prepare students for college, career training, or a well-paying job after high school.

New York State was one of the first states to receive federal funding under the act. The federal government provides funds to help build programs at the state level, which the local communities then take over and run. As of September 1999, New York State had received more than $72 million in federal investments for school-to-work initiatives. By the same date, the state had contributed almost $61 million.

Introducing Apprenticeship Programs

Unlike other programs intended just for vocational or non-college-bound students, school-to-work programs are meant for all students. Hamilton points out that more than half of American students go on to college after high school, but only a little more than half of those come out of college with a degree within five or six years. Among 25- to 30-year-olds as a whole, only 27 percent have four-year college degrees.

The Broome County demonstration project tested whether school-to-work programs could address this problem. The four-year project was based on the German style of apprenticeship, which makes heavy use of what in the United States is called "work-based learning." In Germany, apprentices are enrolled in school part-time, perhaps one or two days per week. The rest of the week they work in an occupation of their choice, which might include traditional crafts, medicine, business, or information technology.

"They are essentially worker-learners," Hamilton says. "Their most important task is to learn the knowledge and the skills that are required in an occupation."

Work-based learning seems particularly suited for one segment of the student population. Hamilton notes that while college-bound students take classroom learning seriously and are able to assimilate information well enough to excel on tests, many others find school impractical and irrelevant. These students feel that classroom assignments are worthless tasks, and they don't see the point of learning geometry or how to write grammatically correct sentences when they don't need those skills to master their after-school jobs.

Benefits to Students

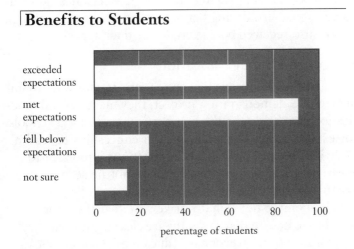

percentage of students

Percentages of employers, parents, and educators who said benefits to students involved in school-to-work had exceeded, met, or fallen below their expectations.

"Perspectives on Progress: The School-to-Work National Customer Dialogues," The Public Forum Institute, September 18, 2000.

Yet it's the limited nature of those after-school jobs that misguides teenagers. They can't see the next level of the occupational hierarchy—jobs that require at least a high school diploma and often an associate's degree, jobs that demand higher communicative skills and sometimes math skills.

"It would be better if we could get these kids out of the classroom for part of the time and put them in a hospital, an auto-repair shop, an insurance company, or a manufacturing plant," Hamilton says. "Make sure that they are not just sweeping floors but are learning to do professional work, in association with people who have higher education and skills. Tell them that if they want to succeed, they have to learn how to do the advanced tasks."

Participants in the Broome County demonstration project began as high school juniors. While still managing to attend school full-time, the students chose to work 10 to 20 hours per week in one of three occupational areas: health care, administration and office technology, and manufacturing and engineering technology. Students like Lisa Wolf, who worked as a human resources clerk at Anitec, a nearby manufacturing facility, during her junior and senior years of high school, also received course credit for their apprenticeships.

Bridges to Higher Education

Although the Hamiltons looked to Germany for ways to implement the demonstration project, they made several modifications to customize the apprenticeships to local schools. For example, they designed the apprenticeships to lead directly into postsecondary education. It was important to the researchers that the work experiences not be seen as an alternative to higher education.

"The point is not only to make sure that the door is left open but to ensure that the paths are clear from what they're doing now into postsecondary education," Hamilton says.

He warns that if high school students choose to leave the education system with only a high school diploma, there's only so far they can go. For example, a student could be a nurse's aide but not a registered nurse, a clerk or secretary but not a systems administrator or accountant.

The Hamiltons also modified the German style of apprenticeship by defining occupations more broadly and by making sure that apprentices rotated among jobs in their places of work. That way they didn't learn only one aspect of a business, and they had a solid basis for deciding whether to specialize in one area or another.

Now ten years after the Hamiltons planted the seed of apprenticeship in Broome County, the program has grown and prospered as a community endeavor. The first apprentices in the demonstration project attest to its effectiveness.

The researchers have followed them since their graduation, and they have found in those young adults a higher level of what they call "career directedness"—meaning that those who worked after high school entered higher-level jobs that were related to the field they chose to explore in high school, and those who went on to a postsecondary school were more likely to major in a field that was related to their career aspirations.

"The apprentices seemed to be able to focus more and to make more rapid progress," Hamilton says.

Designing Effective Programs

The researchers are currently working together on a workplace mentoring study that explores the relationship between the adult teacher and the young learner. Out of interviews with workplace mentors of high school students, the researchers plan to develop materials and guidelines for mentor training and support. The preliminary analyses of the interviews hint at some positive practices among experienced mentors. These include, for example, asking questions to stimulate students' thinking rather than telling them what to do, or emphasizing active problem solving by engaging the young person in answering open-ended puzzles by thinking out loud.

The Hamiltons hope their work will inspire policies and new programs in New York State. Federal grants given to New York State for school-to-work programs are limited in scope and duration—most of the allotted money has already been doled out to the state—and in too many communities the funding was used to maintain previous and arguably superficial efforts, such as field trips and job shadowing.

"Job shadowing is a great introduction as an exploratory experience," Hamilton says. "It gives young people a basis for getting interested in health care or accounting or whatever profession. But if the school-to-work program stops with job shadowing, it's not worthwhile."

West Virginia has used school-to-work as its template for school reform. Like New York State, West Virginia has set academic standards for its students, but rather than using only exams like the Regents in New York State, the state is designing programs that make explicit connections between what students learn in class and what they're going to do in their life work.

Worthy Investments

Although the positive outcomes are hard to pin down because school-to-work hasn't been going on long enough on a large enough scale, there's evidence in Philadelphia, Boston, and Broome County, New York, that students involved in extensive school-to-work programs have achieved higher grades and have gone on to college in greater numbers than their classmates. This disproves the once-held notion that school-to-work programs drive students away from college.

"It has had the opposite effect," Hamilton says.

Lisa Wolf is just one example. After earning a two-year degree from Broome County Community College, she received a B.S. in applied social sciences from Binghamton University in 1999. Now she's an assistant administrator for a nonprofit day care center for parents continuing their education.

But winning school-to-work initiatives won't come at zero cost.

"We found in our demonstration project that successful apprenticeship programs require heavy investments on the part of employers as well as on the part of the school."

"A program that removes . . . [children] from the classroom to gain job skills when they still cannot read, write, add and subtract is indefensibly outrageous."

The Education System Should Not Emphasize Work Skills

Robert W. Schaffer

Robert W. Schaffer contends in the following viewpoint that the federal government's school-to-work program denies high school students a basic liberal-arts education by forcing them to work in menial jobs. According to Schaffer, school-to-work programs were designed to expose high school students to career opportunities and teach them marketable job skills through part-time work experiences. But in Schaffer's opinion, the programs as instituted by states throughout the country are ignoring the dreams and ambitions of children and imposing a one-size-fits-all bureaucratic training program. Schaffer is a Republican congressman from Colorado and serves on the House Education and the Workforce subcommittee on Early Childhood, Youth, and Families.

As you read, consider the following questions:
1. In the author's opinion, why are the job-needs projections of the Workforce Development Boards subject to inaccuracy?
2. Why does Schaffer feel that school-to-work programs are a dangerous shift in education policy?
3. According to Schaffer, what does Mark Wilson of the Heritage Foundation report about the effectiveness of school-to-work policies?

Juan's father phoned his son's high school to find out when he could meet with his tenth-grader's counselor to chart next year's schedule. He bluntly was told that the schedule already had been finalized. Upon receiving a copy in the mail, Juan's father was shocked to discover that the schedule contained no academic courses, but only vocational classes, physical education and released time for a part-time job during school hours. Juan's dream had been to go on to college, but administrators at his school believed he didn't have what it takes to succeed there. Ask Juan.

Less Academics: Good for Students?

Kneisha, a bright-eyed 18-year-old now is being schooled at home. Her parents made the decision to teach her themselves when they realized the local public schools were failing their daughter. This spring, she applied for a summer job. She was told, despite being an outstanding young woman in every way, she couldn't be hired because she hadn't earned her "certificate of initial mastery," and the company was a partner in the region's Workforce Development Board. Ask Kneisha.

Roland wants to go to college and become a teacher. His school district, however, has recommended he study pig farming instead. In fact, school officials told him he must pass a technical pig-farming course if he wants to earn an honors diploma. Ask Roland.

Ask them all: Is [former] President Clinton's School-to-Work program good for students? Then ask every American student who wants to pursue a basic, liberal-arts education that focuses on academics. Ask them how they like being forced into the School-to-Work program, required to leave the classroom to job-shadow and forced to work in menial, entry-level jobs. Ask their parents, too.

School-to-Work (STW) was created by the School-to-Work Opportunities Act of 1994. And, it has worthy objectives. It was designed to introduce students (in some instances as early as kindergarten) to career opportunities and to teach job skills. Like so many federal programs, it has gone tragically awry.

The act provides implementation grants to states. Since

its enactment, all 50 states have received grant money. More than $2 billion has been spent on the program. The states have instituted the program in varying fashion, but federal mandates exist in all the programs. Although federal funding ended on Sept. 30, 2000, most or all states are compelled to continue the program with state funds just as federal planners had hoped.

In a Semiannual Report to Congress, the inspector general of the Department of Education reported on the program in Iowa: "Our audit disclosed that Iowa has initiated numerous actions that, when fully implemented, should ensure the sustainability of the statewide STW initiative after the expiration of STW federal funding, slated for Sept. 30, 2000. Some notable examples include: the enactment of state law, the establishment of supportive policies and strategies and the active interdepartmental participation and leadership of state government."

The report goes on to express some concern about the sustainability of the program and recommends Department of Education collaboration with the state to ensure its continuation. School-to-Work has been designed to survive the end of federal money—and it will.

Federal rules mandate the program be required for all students. School-to-Work is yet another example of Washington bureaucrats and elitists dictating a "one-size-fits-all" program for America's young citizens. It is beyond comprehension that anyone still believes that the same program will fit the needs of schools in Missoula, Montana, as well as in New York City.

Mandates require states to establish partnerships among educators, business groups and labor unions to coordinate regional education programs with workforce requirements. The result is Workforce Development Boards that have been given unprecedented power. For example, they are charged with projecting regional job needs based on one-, five- and 10-year implementation plans. The boards also are required to coordinate school curricula to meet the projected job needs. But ask yourself: How many Webmasters would have been projected five years ago?

The School-to-Work legislation is in part an answer to

the SCANS, or Secretary's Commission on Achieving Necessary Skills, report issued by the Department of Labor. Some of the essential skills that the SCANS report dictates for development in America include such highly subjective (behavioral) skills as self-esteem, honesty, teamwork and sociability. While certainly important character traits, evaluation and tracking of these traits by public schools is ripe for government abuse. Should any shy second-grader receive a grade (which will become part of his permanent record) based upon his sociability?

Opening the Doors to Exploitation

Work-based education requiring performance skills is being touted as the ultimate achievement of today's School-to-Work (STW) reform movement: What are workplace skills? And how do students achieve them?

Students work. In West Virginia, an auto dealer uses his students to wash cars.

In California, a bank uses "honor" students to file. However, one bank manager told me they are pulling out of the program, because graduating "honor" students can't spell well enough to follow directions or file alphabetically.

In New Jersey, students go to Atlantic City casinos to learn how to become card sharks, excuse me, dealers.

We have placed our children at risk of being exploited once more by business. Labor Law violations have already been reported.

A work experience teacher for 20 years recently highlighted her (and other teachers') concerns. In a report to California legislators, she wrote,

> When I started in work experience, labor law enforcement for minors was a priority in the state. Today that is not the case at all. I respectfully request that members of the labor and education committees take their collective heads out of the sand and look at what environment they are producing.

> Harsh economic conditions and welfare reform are also getting parents excited about pushing their student into the work world to bring home some money. They are using School-to-Career as an excuse to opt their student out of academics in favor of part-time jobs.

Karen L. Holgate, "School-to-Work: A Formula for Failure," prepared for the Orange County School Board Hearing, February 11, 1997.

Federal School-to-Work rules also direct states to compile elaborate and detailed computer records on every student. Eventually, schools will be required to transmit detailed student records to potential employers and others. Abuses of privacy are unavoidable.

The architects of School-to-Work hope one day to replace high-school diplomas with "certificates of initial mastery." These certificates will reflect a student's ability to perform job-oriented skills but will not be an indication of broad-based academic knowledge.

Mastering Menial Jobs

School-to-Work is a dangerous shift in education policy in the United States. It moves public education's mission from the transfer of academic knowledge to simply training children (future human resources) for specific jobs. And, most tragically, the job for which it will train a child will have little or nothing to do with that child's dreams, goals and ambitions.

Under School-to-Work, students are expected to learn in the classroom and on the job. Unfortunately, most of the jobs in the program involve menial tasks such as washing cars at the local car dealership and working the grill at the neighborhood burger joint.

While part-time jobs certainly are valuable for high-school students, removing students from the classroom every day to flip burgers is lunacy, at a time when academic achievement in America is declining at a perilous rate.

A Clinton Legacy

The history of the School-to-Work program entails all the intrigue of a Tom Clancy novel. The origins of School-to-Work are found in an 18-page letter dated Nov. 11, 1992, from Marc S. Tucker to Hillary Rodham Clinton. Tucker is the president of the National Center on Education and the Economy. In the letter Tucker tells the soon-to-be first lady of meetings he recently had conducted and pompously writes, "The subject we were discussing was what you and Bill should do now about education, training and labor-market policy." Following the lofty platitudes of the letter's introductory remarks, Tucker spells out the details of the School-to-Work plan. Tucker's manifesto advocates the following:

- A cradle-to-grave, single education system for everyone;
- Redefining postsecondary education to include 11th and 12th grades;
- Converting postsecondary education to an apprenticeship program similar to Germany's system;
- Creating a national system of curriculum, pedagogy, examinations, teacher education and licensure;
- Government funding for dropouts, dislocated workers and the hard-core unemployed;
- Imposition of an education levy on business; and
- Creation of a national system of labor-market boards.

Most of these ideas now are the basis of School-to-Work and its companion legislation, the Workforce Investment Act.

Many states have implemented School-to-Work through executive orders of governors, frequently bypassing state legislators and local officials in the process. This has occurred at a time when citizens are clamoring for a return of most government functions to local control.

A recent national survey by John McLaughlin and Associates asked: To whom do you believe your local public school ultimately should be accountable? Seventy-four percent of survey respondents said parents and the local school district, 12 percent identified state government and only 2 percent listed the federal government.

Devastating Hopes, Dreams, and Goals

Several scholarly institutions have conducted extensive research on School-to-Work. Among them are the American Legislative Exchange Council, or ALEC, and the Heritage Foundation. ALEC has been a leader in alerting state legislators to the perils of this ill-conceived program. Mark Wilson of the Heritage Foundation has written extensively about School-to-Work. He reports that School-to-Work is another redundant federal program that simply has not worked. He points to several studies that demonstrate School-to-Work has been wholly ineffective in raising academic achievement. It also has failed to help participants gain employment—one of its major objectives.

A national leader in School-to-Work research is National

Capital Strategies, or NCS, a research and issues-management firm. NCS has tracked the implementation of School-to-Work from the Tucker letter through the federal legislative process to state-by-state implementation.

Is Clinton's School-to-Work program good for American students? Some elements of it are good for a select few. But any program that devastates children's hopes, dreams and goals is not good for them or for America.

As federal funding expires, states ought to continue the few valuable aspects of the program, such as vocational education. Without federal mandates, states will be free to design their own programs in locally accountable, effective ways.

But states must eliminate the mandatory nature of the program—it should be strictly voluntary. States also must eliminate "certificates of mastery." Assessing and recording highly subjective behavioral skills has no place in a free society. Placing students in middle school on career tracks as they do in Germany and Cuba chills and stifles free choice. We must return a seat at the table to state legislators and local officials.

Finally, we must return our children to basic academic education. A program that removes them from the classroom to gain job skills when they still cannot read, write, add and subtract is indefensibly outrageous.

> "Only workers with the skills needed in the
> new good jobs—the new basic skills—will
> participate in the prosperity accompanying
> economic growth."

Improving Basic Skills Will Benefit Workers

Richard J. Murnane and Frank Levy

Richard J. Murnane and Frank Levy maintain in the follow-ing viewpoint that in order to raise student abilities to the lev-els required by high-wage employers, the education system should emphasize basic skills like mathematics, reading com-prehension, group dynamics, and computer literacy. Having learned these skills, high school graduates, particularly those who do not attend college, will be better equipped to partic-ipate in a technologically demanding job market, in the au-thors' opinion. Richard J. Murnane is professor of economics at the Harvard Graduate School of Education. Frank Levy is professor of economics at the Massachusetts Institute of Technology's Department of Urban Studies and Planning. They are the authors of *Teaching the New Basic Skills*.

As you read, consider the following questions:

1. What explanation do the authors give for the existence of the "schools problem"?
2. In the authors' opinion, why is maintaining the current educational status quo problematic?
3. Why have employers increasingly turned to college graduates to fill job openings, according to Murnane and Levy?

From "A Civil Society Demands Education for Good Jobs," by Richard J. Murnane and Frank Levy, *Educational Leadership*, vol. 54, no. 5 (February 1997), pp. 34–36. Copyright © 1997 Association for Supervision and Curriculum Development. All rights reserved. Reprinted with permission of ASCD.

E ducating students in the new basic skills is the best way to ensure their futures both as wage earners and as participants in a civil society.

We see educating children for a civil society as choosing among three broad alternatives:

• Maintaining the status quo.

• Educating children to participate in the "third sector" envisioned by Jeremy Rifkin.

• Working to raise student skills to the levels now required in good jobs. Readers familiar with our book *Teaching the New Basic Skills* will not be surprised that we support the third alternative. Here we explain our reasoning.

Maintaining the Status Quo

In the 1996 political campaign, candidates frequently argued that U.S. schools had collapsed. Practitioners know this is generally untrue. Judged by standardized test scores, U.S. students are doing a little better in math and no worse in reading than U.S. students did 15 years ago. The "schools problem" exists because over these same years, skill requirements in the labor market have escalated much faster than the schools have improved.

The effect of this is apparent in the median annual earnings of 30-year-old men whose education stopped with a high school diploma: $28,000 in 1979 (in today's dollars) compared with $21,000 today. Young women with high school diplomas are earning somewhat less. Among both sexes, recent college graduates with the weakest skills aren't earning much more. These numbers send a clear signal about the need for stronger skills. But for most parents, the signal arrives only after their child has graduated—after the child has lost contact with teachers and after the parents have lost interest in supporting higher academic standards.

Maintaining the status quo means maintaining this trend: a growing gap between what students learn and what good jobs require. In essence, we will be educating about half of all students for jobs that pay less than a middle-class wage. In this event, maintaining a civil society will be virtually impossible.

The scientist Jeremy Rifkin has outlined a very different kind of future than the one we anticipate [in his book *The*

End of Work: The Decline of the Global Labor Force and the Dawn of the Post-Market Era]. In Rifkin's future, automation will enable most productive work to be performed without workers. Work as we know it will be largely eliminated. We will have to define ourselves through the kinds of third-sector activities that Rifkin discusses [such as meaningful service with neighborhood and community organizations to uphold the values of a civil society].

Rifkin is an imaginative man, but, like all of us, he can only make educated guesses about the future. An educational leader must set priorities under two possible scenarios: Rifkin is right, and Rifkin is wrong.

Suppose schools work to increase traditional student skills (and some "soft" skills we describe below) and Rifkin proves correct. In this case, a slight mismatch may occur because students who have mastered basic mathematics and reading skills may nevertheless not be very good at third-sector activities.

But suppose schools focus exclusively on third-sector activities, largely ignoring the skills we see as critical for the high-paying jobs of the future, and Rifkin proves to be wrong. Then we will have condemned an entire generation to economic inequality beyond what the status quo is producing.

In thinking about these possibilities, keep in mind the current trend toward inequality. The trend is driven in part by rapid technological change in which the rewards of higher productivity are not distributed equally but are distributed largely by supply and demand. Even if the economy moves in the direction that Rifkin describes, there is no guarantee that people who lack the skills to compete will participate in the gains.

Preparing Students for Good Jobs

In *Teaching the New Basic Skills*, we show how high-wage employers are screening job applicants much more carefully than they did 20 years ago. The new basic skills that high-wage employers demand include (1) hard skills (basic mathematics, problem solving, and reading abilities much higher than what almost half of today's high school graduates attain), (2) soft skills (the ability to work in groups with persons of different backgrounds and to make effective oral and written presentations), and (3) the ability to use personal computers to carry out simple tasks, such as word processing.

Of course, many high-wage employers demand more than these new basic skills. But today none demands less.

Suppose our elementary and secondary schools make a commitment to educate children to succeed in a changing job market. Will there be enough good jobs for a larger number of graduates who have mastered the new basic skills? Why focus only on improving K–12 education? Isn't it necessary to graduate from college to get a good job?

Some argue that better schools for all is a dead end. The economy, they say, produces only a certain number of good jobs, so educating too many people too well will only drive down the wages of skilled workers. This argument has merit in the short run. In the long run, however, the economy produces jobs in growing industries as it eliminates jobs in declining industries; but only workers with the skills needed in the new good jobs—the new basic skills—will participate in the prosperity accompanying economic growth.

To understand this, contrast the consequences of technological change in agriculture over the first three quarters of this century with the consequences of recent technological changes in the economy. Farm workers who lost their jobs to mechanization experienced significant hardships. However, most of them found jobs that paid more than those they left because they could do the jobs that were becoming increasingly available in manufacturing. For example, work on automobile assembly lines was hard and dirty, but it did not require skills that farm workers lacked. As a result, most of the displaced farm workers found new jobs that allowed them to improve their standard of living along with most other Americans.

In contrast, many Americans displaced by technological change today find that they lack the skills to find good jobs in the parts of the economy that are growing. As a result, they are not participating in the fruits of economic growth. Their earnings fall further and further below the earnings of workers who possess the skills that are in demand. This is likely to continue for workers who lack the new basic skills.

While the real earnings of male high school graduates

plummeted over the last 15 years, those of college graduates held steady. Some interpret this as evidence that the key to improving the earnings of the next generation of workers is to send all students to college. To see why this is an inappropriate interpretation of the evidence, consider two alternative reasons why high-wage employers have increasingly turned to college graduates and away from high school graduates. The first is that high-wage employers increasingly need the advanced skills learned in college. The second is that they need the new basic skills, and students go to college to prove to employers that they have these skills—skills that may be learned in high school but that a high school diploma does not guarantee.

To distinguish these two interpretations, consider these questions from a basic mathematics test given to high school seniors:

Directions. Each problem consists of two quantities, one in Column A and one in Column B. Compare the two quantities and circle the letter A if the quantity in Column A is greater; B if the quantity in Column B is greater; C if the two quantities are equal; or D if the size relationship cannot be determined from the information given.

Flunking the Test: Basic Math Stumps Many High School Graduates

Column A

1. Length represented by 3 inches on a scale of 4 feet to an inch
2. Q such that:
   $$\frac{1}{Q} = \frac{3}{4}$$
3. Cost per apple at a rate of 3 apples for \$.50

Column B

1. A length of 12 feet
2. P such that:
   $$\frac{1}{P} = \frac{4}{3}$$
3. Cost per apple at a rate of \$2 per dozen apples

Richard J. Murnane and Frank Levy, *Educational Leadership*, February 1997.

Answering these questions requires mathematics that virtually all high school students have been taught by the 9th grade, if not earlier. Yet almost half of high school students graduate without mastery of these skills.

In writing *Teaching the New Basic Skills*, we analyzed two U.S. Department of Labor surveys that gave these questions (and similar questions on literacy) to high school seniors. Each survey then followed the young people over time as some went to college and others didn't. When the young people reached their mid-20s, the researchers collected information on the jobs they held and the wages they earned. One survey covered the 1970s and the other covered the 1980s—years that bracketed the rapid increase in the college earnings premium.

With our colleague John Willett, we used these surveys to analyze the growth in the college earnings premium. The results show that when wages are adjusted for the basic skills a student knew in high school, half of the growth in the men's college wage premium and all of the growth in the women's college wage premium are eliminated.

These results mean that high-wage employers increasingly hire college graduates because they want workers with the new basic skills, and many high school graduates who did not go to college lack these skills. Hiring college graduates solves the problem of finding workers with these skills, but college is a very expensive employment agency. If more high school students without basic skills mastery went to college, the earnings of college graduates would fall unless colleges invested more heavily in remedial education—an expensive proposition. But if all students left high school with the new basic skills and were able to demonstrate mastery of these skills to employers, the differential between the earnings of high school graduates and college graduates would be much smaller.

The New Basic Skills and Civil Society

Americans may find it difficult to agree on the details of a curriculum to prepare students to participate fully in a civil society. But surely a civil society must be one in which graduates of the nation's schools are able to earn enough to support children. This will happen only when all students graduate with mastery of the new basic skills. Consequently, emphasis on these skills must be at the center of education for a civil society.

The new basic skills are not only necessary for economic prosperity in a changing economy. They are also important to citizenship in a pluralistic democracy. The ability to work productively with people from different backgrounds is not only important on the job. It is also important in the voluntary activities that Jeremy Rifkin describes. This is equally true for the ability to communicate effectively, both orally and in writing. For this reason we see our definition of education for a civil society as agreeing in some respects with Rifkin's.

We disagree with Rifkin, however, about the future of the economy. Whereas he predicts a decline in earnings opportunities, we interpret current economic data—especially the highest employment-to-population ratio in the last 50 years—as evidence that there will be jobs in the foreseeable future and good jobs for workers who have mastered the new basic skills.

To see the relevance of these skills to the civil society, suppose the increasing obsolescence of the education provided in most U.S. schools is allowed to continue. The children of the wealthy and the clever will cluster in privileged schools—public and private—that do emphasize the new basic skills. These children will get a good education and good jobs. The majority of other children will compete for what is left—hardly a vision for a civil society.

> *"It is illogical to blame elementary and high school educators for failing to teach workers specialized skills. . . . The real problem is the absence of an apprenticeship program."*

Improving Basic Skills Will Not Benefit Workers

Steve Kangas

In the following viewpoint, Steve Kangas argues that American workers are graduating from public high schools with more than enough fundamental education to perform their jobs. According to Kangas, a glut of college graduates on the labor market has led to a displacement effect in which high school graduates must compete against overqualified workers for employment. What is needed, in the author's opinion, is not more basic skills education, but apprenticeship programs that teach specialized job skills to the four-fifths of Americans who do not attend college. Before his death in 1999, Kangas maintained a website responding to conservative critics of liberalism on a number of social policy issues.

As you read, consider the following questions:

1. In 1990, what percentage of all college graduates were unemployed or in jobs that did not require a college degree, according to Kangas?
2. How does Kangas respond to critics who claim that the public education system is not teaching the skills required in a high-tech economy?
3. What advantages do apprenticeship programs have over on-the-job training, in the author's opinion?

Reprinted from "Myth: American Graduates Don't Have the Skills Needed for a High-Tech Economy," by Steve Kangas, published at www.huppi.com/kangaroo/ L-collegeglut.htm.

Many critics of American public education argue that too many students are graduating without the skills needed for a high-tech economy. Employers tell anecdotal horror stories about job applicants who cannot read or write or perform their jobs adequately. Fortunately, these criticisms describe the exceptions, not the rule.

In fact, there is a glut of college graduates on the labor market. In 1993, one-third of all 1991 and 1992 college graduates held jobs that did not require a college degree. As for *all* college graduates, in 1990, 20 percent either held jobs that did not require a college degree or were unemployed. That was up from 18 percent in 1979 and 11 percent in 1968.

Overqualified, Underemployed

The glut is so serious that competition among college students to enter graduate school has reached a fever pitch. In 1996, for example, 46,968 students competed for 16,200 openings in medical schools across the country. At law schools, 70,900 students applied for 43,000 openings. Similar gluts exist in virtually all fields. Even the lucky few who graduate with doctorates find themselves competing for too few jobs that require their degrees. According to a 1995 study by Stanford University and the Rand Corporation, universities turn out "25 percent more doctorates in science and engineering than the U.S. economy can absorb."

With too many overqualified workers at the top, a displacement effect runs down the entire job ladder. The best high school graduates who seek non-professional jobs find themselves competing with college graduates. These competent high school graduates are then bumped down, to compete for even lower jobs.

What this means is that the vast majority of American workers have more than enough fundamental education to perform their jobs. In 1989, a survey called "The Commission on the Skills of the American Workforce" questioned American employers on the education of their workers. The researchers found that over 80 percent of American employers were satisfied with the education of their newly hired employees. Only 5 percent expected that their employees would require further basic training or education.

International Comparisons

And how does American education stack up against that of other nations? At the college level, the U.S. is the most highly educated society in the world. At the elementary and high school level, the U.S. has a mixed record.

Adding the figures in the first two columns of Table 1 shows how well each nation educates its non-college work-force. For example, the U.S. gives 69 percent of its society either an elementary or high school education, although in Italy it's 94 percent, France, 84 percent, etc. On the other hand, the U.S. also sees more of its students through high school than most other countries, which have unusually high dropout rates even in elementary school. So, on the whole, the U.S. produces more highly educated workers than any other nation.

Another criticism is that the public education system isn't teaching students the skills that will be required in our rapidly changing high-tech economy. Apple Computer Chairman John Sculley once complained to [former] Presi-

Table 1. Educational attainment of persons aged 25 to 64 years old, percent by country, 1992

Country	Primary Only	Secondary Also	College Also
United States	16%	53	24
Netherlands	42	37	21
Canada	29	30	15
Denmark	41	40	13
Germany	18	60	12
Norway	21	54	12
Sweden	30	46	12
United Kingdom	32	49	11
Finland	39	43	10
France	48	36	10
Switzerland	19	60	8
Italy	72	22	6

Organization for Economic Cooperation and Development, *Education at a Glance*, 1992.

dent Clinton that "We're still trapped in a K–12 public education system which is preparing our young people for jobs that just don't exist anymore."

But this criticism doesn't hold water. With relatively minor spending increases, educators have been able to add enough computers to elementary school classrooms that 54 percent of all students now use them. At present, this is an even greater percentage than those who use computers on the job.

The U.S. does, however, fail to train its future workers in a way that most other prosperous nations do not. Other nations have extensive apprenticeship programs for workers who do not go on to college. The success of these publicly funded programs is considerable, and many foreign entrepreneurs have scratched their heads over why the U.S. has not adopted them.

The problem is this: lower education is general education, teaching the fundamentals that are universally needed by all citizens, regardless of their future jobs. But at the higher levels, education becomes increasingly specialized. In the U.S., true specialization in a particular job field does not really occur until college. Yet, roughly four-fifths of all Americans do not attend college, even though they will be choosing job specialties as well, and have just as much need for specialized training. Other nations solve this problem through apprenticeship programs. By contrast, blue-collar workers in the U.S. must struggle through on-the-job training.

On-the-job training has many serious drawbacks. First, simply knowing a job is insufficient for a manager to train someone else in it. Training and educating others efficiently, easily and completely is a high skill, one that the majority of managers fail to master. Not surprisingly, most do it poorly. The advantage of a formal apprenticeship program is that it can be designed and taught by experts.

Second, on-the-job training works well for simple jobs, but in an increasingly high-tech world, it may become too lengthy and expensive for companies to accept. In that case, businessmen and educators often engage in a lot of finger-pointing, trying to blame each other for the workers' lack of skills. Educators blame businessmen for not supporting apprenticeship programs, and businessmen blame educators for inadequate primary and secondary education. The latter charge is fallacious, however, because elementary and high school are for general education, not specialized education.

Many companies are learning the value of privately funded apprenticeship programs. Here is a success story reported in *The American Prospect:*

> Ten years ago, Harley Shaiken began to study Ford Motor Company's new engine plant in Chihuahua, Mexico. Initially, he believed that Ford's gamble to save on labor costs in Mexico (where 6 years of school is the norm) would fail. Manufacturing engines is a sophisticated operation, with machine tolerances of one ten-thousandth of an inch. Coordination between production workers and technicians is essential. Yet while Ford required only 9 years of education for new hires in its Chihuahua facility, it has become the world's most productive engine plant and is now Ford's sole North American engine source.

> Ford enrolled Mexican school dropouts in a 4-to-12-week technology institute program covering gasoline engines, mechanical drawing, and mathematics. New hires learned to tear down and reassemble an engine. Once on the job, they were rotated every 3 to 6 months to new tasks, so skills would be broadened further.

> As the Chihuahua plant matured, Ford hired workers with less schooling and relied even more on its own training. As skilled technicians left, Ford replaced them with production workers promoted and trained from within, as required by Ford's Mexican union contract.

Apprenticeship programs are clearly successful, but one of the controversies involved with them is who should pay for them. Some argue that businesses should pay for them, since they are the ones who benefit from them. (In economic terms, this is called "internalizing the externality.") Others argue that government should pay for them, as a public investment in the success of our economy. (This already describes our public education system, from kindergarten through college.) There are good arguments on both sides of this debate. But the key point here is that it is illogical to blame elementary and high school educators for failing to teach workers specialized skills, since that is not their function. The real problem is the absence of an apprenticeship program.

"The need to develop a comprehensive, more-effective training strategy remains."

Job Training Programs Should Be Expanded

Anthony P. Carnevale

In the following viewpoint, Anthony P. Carnevale asserts that job training programs are an effective means of reducing unemployment and increasing workers' adaptability in a changing economy. Job training provides workers with the skills to advance out of low-wage jobs and encourages equal access to good jobs for all Americans, in Carnevale's opinion. According to the author, public policy should place more emphasis on education and job training and less on "work-first" policies for those who do not pursue a college education. Carnevale is vice president for public leadership at the Educational Testing Service.

As you read, consider the following questions:
1. By how much did federal support for job training programs fall between 1978 and 1999, according to Carnevale?
2. How does the author support his assertion that tight labor markets are unlikely to close the earnings gap among males?
3. In Carnevale's opinion, why has more public action not been taken to increase job training programs?

Excerpted from "Beyond Consensus: Much Ado About Job Training," by Anthony P. Carnevale, *Brookings Review*, vol. 17, no. 4 (Fall 1999), p. 40. Reprinted with permission.

Nearly everyone agrees that training is a valuable tool for reducing unemployment, underemployment, and income disparity as well as for increasing adaptability in the global economy. Publicly sponsored training appeals to us particularly because it mixes individual responsibility with collective compassion. Yet training consistently looms far larger in policy talk than in public budgets.

To some extent, training gets the budget share it deserves. Much rhetoric on training overpromises. The notion that "If we train, then the jobs will come" is shaky at best. Still, we have learned a great deal, both from our successes and from our failures in training policy, over the past three decades. On the whole, little of what we have learned disturbs the initial intuition that training policy, effectively designed, can be a useful economic and social policy tool. And, after 30 years at it, we know how to design effective training programs.

How We Got Here

Ever since the Kennedy round of global trade agreements in the 1960s, training programs for workers dislocated by changes in federal trade, environmental, space, and defense policies have been a staple of federal legislation. Disadvantaged youth and adults became federal training clients when Michael Harrington discovered those "other Americans" not sharing in the general prosperity in the 1960s and again when stagflation and the baby boomers hit labor markets in the 1970s. When economic restructuring and downsizing became genuine concerns in the 1980s, middle-income working people joined the laundry list of eligible recipients for federal training—a list fast outstripping available funds.

By the mid-1980s, a "new economy" was emerging; work was becoming the primary integrative force in society for both men and women. It was generally agreed that if everyone were at work in a fully mobilized society, everyone would be included not only in the economy but in the polity and culture as well. According to the new orthodoxy, labor market programs needed to focus less on income support when workers became unemployed and more on "reemployment" policies. Economists also began reporting the growing importance of skill in explaining increasing differences in earnings. Despite the rhetorical emphasis on training, however, money for federal training programs declined during the 1980s—from 0.12 percent to 0.09 percent of gross domestic product (GDP). And the trend continued. Federal training dollars fell from $24 billion in 1978 to $7 billion in 1999.

Still, we kept talking about the importance of training. In the 1992 presidential election campaign, Bill Clinton proposed to supplant the crazy quilt of small programs targeted on the economically disadvantaged and dislocated workers with a new training system that would provide universal eligibility. The new system was to include three elements—a "school-to-work-apprenticeship" program, a beefed-up employer training agenda, and new skill standards for private-sector jobs—to be complemented by an investment program to "rebuild America" and by "high-performance work systems" to encourage employers to retrain workers and reorganize work systems to favor high-skilled workers. . . .

Clinton's ambitious federal training agenda has hardly reared its head since. During his second term, the emphasis shifted toward expanding grants, loans, and tax credits for postsecondary education. Training policy fell back into the familiar tug-of-war between expert opinion and the interests of agencies and providers over declining resources.

Not to Worry?

Meanwhile, although a booming economy seems to have banished our unemployment problems, helped ease income disparity, and made training seem superfluous, the need to develop a comprehensive, more-effective training strategy remains.

The connections between general economic prosperity and the lives of ordinary working people remain tenuous. Tight labor markets alone are unlikely to close the earnings gap, because on-the-job training ladders out of low-wage jobs are collapsing as entry-level manufacturing jobs decline. The ratio of the 90th to the 10th percentile among male wage earners, which increased from 3.59 percent in 1973 to 4.52 percent in 1993, declined only to 4.47 percent in 1997—closing only 6 percent of the opening gap. In 1996,

3.5 million American workers worked full-time, full-year, and 4.3 million worked at least 27 weeks and nonetheless lived in poor families. And skill barriers make it increasingly difficult for people to work their way out of poverty. Thirty-nine percent of Americans in the labor force have skills below the minimum competency established by the Organization for Economic Cooperation and Development.

In addition—although no one wants to mention it—we may not have banished economic cycles. At the moment, everything is "just right" in the Goldilocks economy, but the bears may show up eventually. "Generation Y" may not be as easy as the smaller "Generation X" was to integrate into the labor force. In our fully mobilized work-first society, both long-term and short-term economic fortunes are more connected to labor markets, and labor market success is more connected to skill acquisition. At the same time, unemployment, whether individual or mass, is longer-term and more structural, and structural barriers are most often skill barriers. And if skill is the question, training will likely be part of the answer.

Another strong argument for continuing to press for effective public training programs is built on the fundamental belief that all individuals matter and each matters equally. As the world's most diverse postindustrial nation, the United States sets the highest standards for inclusion, both as an extension of its democratic principles and as a recognition that economic differences threaten bedrock institutions. And inclusion begins with universal—and equal—access to good jobs. Training is one way to encourage access, especially for minorities, women, and low-income families.

Restarting the Training Dialogue

Why has our apparent consensus on training not resulted in concerted public action? One obvious explanation is that while support for training and other active labor market policies in the United States has always been wide, it has not been deep. The failure to bring boutique training policies to universal scale tracks to the political and financial barriers to expanding the welfare state beyond educational guarantees for the young and income and health-care security for a steadily increasing elderly population.

The fragmentation of U.S. labor markets also makes a broad-based training policy difficult. Training, like wages, pensions, health care, and other work-related aspects of the social order, is organized around particular occupations and industries and is, therefore, hard to conduct on a large scale. The fragmentation of education and social welfare benefit levels makes it difficult to switch to a more homogenous national benefit level. (The health-care debate is a case in point.) As a result, government provision of work-related training and other benefits tends to focus only on those who do not have access to private coverage. Thus, private citizens—who might pay for but not benefit from such programs—do not typically support them.

Minimalist government, in combination with fragmented labor markets, leads to fragmented public programs. With few universal programs, support for funding is built one program and one interest group at a time. And our inability to integrate education, training, and social welfare programs means each is less effective than it could be. Our fiscal and administrative federalism, too, further confounds attempts to address fragmentation. Europeans were more successful with their training systems in the 1980s not only because they spent more—anywhere from five to ten times as much as the United States—but because their training programs were embedded in more cohesive systems of individual support.

At their most profound level, the fragmentation in our policies results in a disconnect between training policies and employment policies. Notwithstanding the occasional debate over "industrial policy," employment policy has long since moved beyond explicit programs to the reified world of fiscal and monetary policies. Indeed, when our training and employment policies are related, the relationship is perverse. We provide the most training for workers when private jobs are unavailable. And when jobs do exist, when training would likely have significant positive effects, we retreat from training—in part because training programs didn't provide work when there wasn't any.

The policy divide between employment and training reflects a similar disconnect in the popular consciousness.

Workforce preparation in the United States is largely driven by general education or through vocational certification in two-year colleges or technical schools, not by training. Total spending on postsecondary education is more than $200 billion annually compared with $7 billion for training.

Correcting Labor Market Woes

[Why] should there be concern over improving the employment and training system? The answer lies in the currently troubling outcomes in the American labor market that, at least in principle, are remediable by an effective employment and training system:

• Increasingly unequal wages. The bottom has fallen out of the labor market for workers with a high school education or less. The reasons are not understood well, but virtually all observers agree that augmenting the skills of persons on the lowest rung of the ladder is an important part of any solution.

• Difficulties some youth have in settling down. Most young people successfully navigate the school-to-work transition and obtain "adult" jobs by their late 20s. However, 20–30% experience serious problems in settling into adult jobs.

• Racial disparities remain sharp in the labor market. In 1994, for instance, 63% of whites between 16 and 64 were employed, compared to 56% of blacks and 59% of Hispanics. Respective employment figures for teenagers were 47%, 24%, and 33%. Considerably larger proportions of African-Americans and Hispanics work at poverty-level wages than do whites.

• Adult displacement. The American labor market has become increasingly turbulent. Permanently displaced workers face an average earnings loss of some 20%.

Paul Osterman, *USA Today Magazine*, January 1998.

Expert data support the popular view. In the United States, the earnings returns from education, job training, and access to technology tend to be sequential, complementary, and cumulative. Those who have more schooling have more access to jobs with the most formal or informal training as well as access to more technology, which means they earn more money. And, yes, employers do train. They spend about $60 billion a year in formal training and another $180 billion in informal training, but the training extends to the 20 percent of their personnel who already have the most education. That spending will grow in the future. As the college-educated workforce increases between now and 2006, employers will have to spend another $15 billion just to maintain their current training commitments to their college-educated workers. But the least-educated workers are unlikely to get more employer-provided training. . . .

What Next?

As the the 1990s came to a close, public policy promised "college first" for the most advantaged and "work first" at hard labor for everybody else. Work-first policies are consistent with our growing need for mobilization and our commitment to work, and to inclusion through work, but they overlook the decline in the demand for unskilled labor and the limited mobility out of unskilled jobs. Simply put, most jobs do not provide training of any kind, and individuals without postsecondary skills don't get the jobs that do.

Whither training? The first step seems obvious. We need to continue to struggle with how to integrate social welfare, workforce development, and education policy—a job that only presidents and governors can do. We should formally recognize the silent partnership between education, training, and social policy that has already made postsecondary Pell Grants the universal workforce development voucher for adults, who already receive as much as $3 billion from those grants. The use of Pell Grants to achieve social welfare and employment policy goals has fallen off since the shift in emphasis to "work first." But 476,000 Aid to Families with Dependent Children recipients and their dependents used Pell Grants as recently as 1997. And in 1992, the last year for which data were available, 75,000 dislocated workers used Pell Grants, many in combination with federal student loans.

Making the role of postsecondary education more explicit in social policy and workforce development policy is not enough, however. By 2015 up to 3 million new 18- to 24-year-old traditional students will enter U.S. colleges and universities each year. Under that pressure, postsecondary education will have few incentives to serve the special needs of nontraditional [vocational] students. Social welfare and workforce development agencies must overcome the fragmentation in public services for special populations by customizing a broad range of services, including referrals to postsecondary institutions, to meet the complex needs of individual clients on a case-by-case basis.

Outcomes should drive our workforce development system. Employer wage records, already reported quarterly for all civilian workers, should be the cornerstone of the accountability system, as they already are in states like Florida and Washington. Tax credits would encourage employers to train their first-level supervisors and nonsupervisory employees. Increasing credits for employers who use state-certified education and training institutions would strengthen relationships between certified training providers and employers.

Realistically speaking, the key policy issue for the United States is the long-standing disconnect between training policies and jobs. Although a national dialogue on job creation seems superfluous now, the next debate over jobs is only as far away as the next recession. When work disappears in a work-first policy world, we will have to decide whether to warehouse workers until jobs return or make another try at connecting employment and training policies.

A serious policy dialogue that links training with job creation will have to be about services because that is where the good jobs are growing. Almost all of America's impressive job creation in high-wage services has come in private business services. An employment and training strategy for the postindustrial era would invest in undercapitalized critical social services. We might, for example, provide serious training in child care. Such training, along with new tax-incentive programs and regulation, could encourage more people to enter a private child-care market that would be governed by rigorous professional certification. We would thereby promote the common weal and create a whole new wave of high-paid, high-skilled jobs.

Now That All the Poor Are Deserving

The likelihood that we will move beyond the current superficial consensus on training policy to concerted public action will depend on economic, social, and moral considerations.

. . . Training may be part of a new solution to link national competitiveness in the yo-yo global economy to the needs of individual workers. Tight labor markets and universal training policies would be a unique mix in American politics. But this time, full employment feels different. Even if job tenure stays put in the official data, the public expectation for job security is clearly not being met. Training is no substitute for a good job, but it might help get one and, barring more aggressive employment policies, it is all the government can offer. For the same reasons, training policies are a sure part of the consolation package for affected workers the next time we decide to save the odd endangered bird, beetle, or trade bill. And if the American job machine doesn't produce a sufficient quantity or quality of jobs, political pragmatists will reach first for training and then, eventually, for employment policy solutions.

The social and moral impetus for training policy depends on our tolerance for income inequality in our diverse society and the strength of our commitment to social mobility. Post-welfare reform work-first policies have exposed the issue of working poverty. Now all the poor are "deserving," and training programs are one way to make work pay.

"Most government job training programs have been shown to be ineffective."

Traditional Job Training Programs Are Ineffective

Anita Hattiangadi

Anita Hattiangadi claims in the following viewpoint that the "training first" approach to helping unemployed U.S. workers find jobs is ineffective. Instead of placing participants in jobs, "training first" often ends up moving hard-to-serve individuals with limited skills from training program to training program, in Hattiangadi's opinion. Hattiangadi is an economist with the Employment Policy Foundation, a research and educational foundation that provides policymakers and the public with economic analysis and commentary on U.S. employment policies.

As you read, consider the following questions:
1. By what percentage have welfare rolls dropped since the signing of the welfare reform law, according to the author?
2. Aside from government, to whom does Hattiangadi give credit for the success of welfare-to-work initiatives?
3. What government job training program, replaced by the Workforce Investment Act, failed to improve the employment and earnings of its participants, in the author's opinion?

Reprinted, with permission, from "'Work First' vs. 'Training First': Does the Workforce Investment Act Reflect the Lessons Learned from Welfare Reform?" by Anita Hattiangadi, *Employment Policy Foundation Fact & Fallacy*, vol. 4, no. 10, (October 1998).

On August 22, 1998, [former] President Clinton and the Department of Health and Human Services (HHS) marked the two-year anniversary of the Personal Responsibility and Work Opportunity Act, *i.e.*, "welfare reform." The legislation, which has resulted in an extensive revamping of the U.S. welfare system, reflected a dramatic shift in public social policy towards a "work first" approach to helping disadvantaged individuals and away from the traditional "training first" approaches followed in the past. Coincidentally, two weeks earlier, the [former] President signed the Workforce Investment Act of 1998—an attempt to reform government job training programs. This legislation perpetuates a "training first" approach to helping the disadvantaged.

The Success of "Work First" Approaches

In recent years, public opinion has favored "work first" approaches to helping disadvantaged individuals. The welfare reform law first reflected this changed focus. The law requires caseworkers to help welfare recipients seek and obtain employment rather than automatically assigning them to a job training or education program. States are also required to have certain shares of the welfare population working by specified deadlines and allow only a small share of the population to be exempted from work requirements.

Preliminary results suggest that the "work first" strategy has been quite effective. Welfare rolls peaked in 1994, but have dropped by 32 percent nationally since the signing of welfare reform in 1996. In some states, rolls have fallen even more dramatically; the number of welfare recipients is down by 71 percent in Wisconsin and 52 percent in Florida. Despite claims that the law would result in mass destitution, there is new evidence that individuals leaving the rolls are finding jobs. HHS reports that 1.7 million adults who were on welfare in 1996 were working in March 1997.

Evidence from welfare-to-work programs in several states suggests that programs with a "work first" approach and some limited job training have improved the employment and earnings of former welfare recipients. Portland, Oregon's program assigned most individuals to job search activities and sanctioned individuals for non-compliance, but those who could not find a job were allowed several months of basic education, job or motivational training, self-esteem courses, drug and alcohol treatment, or subsidized work experience. Still, a recent evaluation found that program participants were seven times more likely to engage in job search activities than those in the traditional welfare program. Furthermore, individuals in the program were more likely to get jobs than those in the traditional welfare program and earned about 35 percent more than their traditional program counterparts over two years.

The largest county welfare-to-work program in the country, Los Angeles County's Jobs-First GAIN program, had evolved in recent years from a provider of relatively high-cost educational services to a "work first" program. Preliminary results show that after six months 43 percent of the Jobs-First participants were employed, compared to 32 percent of individuals in the traditional welfare program. During the same period, earnings for the Jobs-First group outpaced the traditional group by about 46 percent.

Studies in several states also reflect successes. A recent study in Indiana found that 64 percent of former welfare recipients were working after 18 months and a study in South Carolina found 59 percent of welfare leavers were working after six months. In Maryland, about a third of recipients either had found work or had outside income to put them above set income ceilings for welfare receipt, and more than half had worked at least part of the quarter following their exit from welfare.

Certainly, attempts to remove recipients from the welfare rolls have been helped by a booming economy, but much of this progress has been a result of the strong participation of the business community and private service providers in welfare-to-work initiatives. Corporate programs, most using private or public-private cooperative intermediary organizations for screening and training, are proving effective in helping welfare recipients move into jobs. A survey by the Welfare-to-Work Partnership estimates that 135,000 former welfare recipients were hired by U.S. companies during 1997 and 1998, many of them by small businesses. Several larger companies have done substantial hiring—Burger

King and United Parcel Service each hired over ten thousand former welfare recipients during 1997 and 1998. These programs are demonstrating that the "work first" approach combined with guidance from the private sector can succeed in moving individuals from welfare to work.

A Return to the "Training First" Approach?

Faced with these successes, [former] President Clinton signed the Workforce Investment Act. The legislation will consolidate 60 of over 163 federal job training programs and will provide federal funding of job training through block grants to states and localities. In view of the success of "work first," there are good reasons to be skeptical of whether the measure will remedy the present shortcomings of government-provided job training.

The Act is a less extensive overhaul of the present system than was proposed by the failed legislation of the 104th Congress, the Workforce and Career Development Act of 1996. That Act would have consolidated more than 100 programs into a single block grant; the Workforce Investment Act consolidates about 60 programs into three block grants. Last Congress's effort would have also consolidated most funding streams while the new Act maintains separate funding streams for certain groups, such as veterans and dislocated workers. Furthermore, unlike the earlier legislation which proposed the closure of 10 underperforming Job Corps centers, the new law basically leaves Job Corps untouched. Job Corps is a residential job training program for disadvantaged youth which had an average per person cost in 1996 of over $15,000 and total costs of over $1 billion annually.

The legislation reflects and perpetuates the "training first" approach in the face of good evidence that traditional job training programs do not work. The Job Training Partnership Act (JTPA), previously the largest federal employment training program, lacked measurable success in improving the employment and earnings of many segments of the disadvantaged population. A 1996 long-term control group evaluation of the program by the General Accounting Office reported that adults experienced some increase in wages and employment following program completion, but after five years no statistically significant effects on wages or employment remained. (See Graph.) Employment rates for adults were actually lower five years after program completion than in the year prior to assignment. Youths completing the JTPA program showed no significant positive effects in their employment or earnings in any of the years analyzed.

Effect of the Job Training Partnership Act (JTPA) Program on the Employment of Adult Women

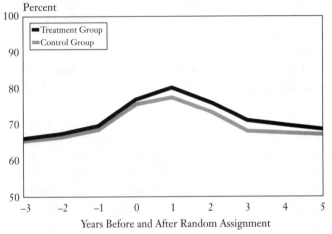

Job Training Partnership Act: Long-Term Earnings and Employment Outcomes, GAO/HEHS-96-40. (March 4, 1996).

In fact, most attempts by the government to train workers have been unsuccessful. Numerous studies show that government job training programs are redundant, costly, and produce limited results at best. Because taxpayers spend over $20 billion on employment and training programs each year, these results are quite discouraging.

Is the "Training First" Focus of Job Training Misdirected?

The failure of job training to live up to the expectations of policymakers and the public, however, is in large part the result of the misdirected focus of job training efforts. The "training first" approach often results in individuals continually moving from one training program to another with little emphasis on actually getting a job. Furthermore, most government job training programs have been shown to be ineffective. Research shows that on-the-job training is much more effective than any classroom-based job training.

Additionally, traditional job training programs target hard-to-serve individuals who often lack labor market experience and have only limited skills. Job training will likely produce much more positive results if it is focused on the more trainable group of disadvantaged individuals—those who may actually realize higher wages or better employment prospects as a result of such training. For these workers, vouchers can make the delivery of these services more efficient and effective. As a nod in that direction, the Workforce Investment Act does provide "individual training accounts" for job training, but there is little detail provided so it remains to be seen how they are implemented in practice.

The Workforce Investment Act of 1998 attempts to reform the failed federal job training system in the U.S. Unfortunately, it maintains a "training first" focus which evidence shows is unlikely to improve the employment and earnings of disadvantaged individuals. Recent evaluations show that "work first" approaches have been more successful in helping individuals to find employment and increase their earnings. What remains to be seen is whether new job training programs implemented under the Workforce Investment Act will be redirected to a "work first" focus currently driving welfare-to-work efforts.

Ultimately, no welfare-to-work or job training program, no matter how well-designed or administered, can erase the effects of an inadequate educational background. As the economic rewards from education increase, those with inadequate basic skills are left further behind. Consequently, education reform is key to ensuring that future generations do not become "disadvantaged" in the first place.

Periodical Bibliography

The following articles have been selected to supplement the diverse views presented in this chapter. Addresses are provided for periodicals not indexed in the *Readers' Guide to Periodical Literature*, the *Alternative Press Index*, the *Social Sciences Index*, or the *Index to Legal Periodicals and Books*.

Norish Adams and Janette Gerdes	"Should Today's Education Be Relevant to Tomorrow's Job Market?" *NEA Today*, January 1999.
Anthony P. Carnevale and Donna Desrochers	"Training in the Dilbert Economy," *Training and Development*, December 1999.
Lynne Cheney	"Limited Horizons," *New York Times*, February 3, 1998.
Bill Clinton	"Remarks on Signing the School-to-Work Opportunities Act of 1994," *Weekly Compilation of Presidential Documents*, May 9, 1994.
Robert C. Fellmeth	"Capacity of Colleges Is Getting Short Shrift," *Los Angeles Times*, September 12, 1999.
Robert J. Gitter and Markus Scheuer	"U.S. and German Youths: Unemployment and the Transition from School to Work," *Monthly Labor Review*, March 1997.
Alison Gopnik	"Children Need Childhood, Not Vocational Training," *New York Times*, December 24, 2000.
David L. Gray	"Shaping America's Workforce for the New Millennium," *Education*, Summer 2000.
James J. Heckman	"Doing It Right: Job Training and Education," *The Public Interest*, Spring 1999.
James Hettinger	"The Buck Stops Soon," *Techniques*, November 1998.
Amy Kaslow	"Skills Shortage Threatens U.S. Competitiveness," *HR Focus*, November 1998.
Alice Laplante	"Sowing Seeds of Success," *Computerworld*, February 1, 1999.
Richard J. Murnane and Frank Levy	"Clinton Is Half-Right on Schools," *New York Times*, February 17, 1997.
Paul Osterman	"Reforming Employment and Training Policies," *USA Today Magazine*, January 1998.
Robert J. Samuelson	"Stupid Students, Smart Economy?" *Washington Post*, March 12, 1998.

Phyllis Schlafly   "Education Loses in School-to-Work Plan," *Washington Times*, March 6, 1997.

Philip Siekman   "Tapping the Last Big Labor Pool," *Fortune*, September 4, 2000.

Jodi Wilgoren   "College Education Seen as Essential," *New York Times*, May 4, 2000.

Should the Government Intervene in the Job Market?

Chapter Preface

To alleviate widespread unemployment during the Great Depression of the 1930s, the federal government under President Franklin D. Roosevelt embarked on the first large-scale intervention into the private economy with the New Deal and its public-jobs programs. The success of the New Deal at easing unemployment remains the subject of debate, but Roosevelt's intervention established a new role for government as overseer of the economy and promoter of full employment.

Since Roosevelt's time, government has expanded its reach into the private economy with welfare and job training programs for the unemployed and minimum wage legislation. Critics of government spending to reduce unemployment contend that such policies siphon capital from the private economy through high taxes and other regulatory costs. In addition, say critics, such policies drain labor from the private sector by placing people in inefficient jobs for which there is no demand, depriving the market of the flexibility needed to respond to economic changes. In the opinion of Donald J. Senese, a former associate professor of history at Radford University, "[Government programs] reward 'nonwork' at the expense of the productive sector."

Supporters of government intervention argue that controls must be imposed on the free market to minimize the negative effects of unemployment. Says Cindy Wiggins, senior researcher in social and economic policy for the Canadian Labour Congress, "The free market, if left to itself, would not act in the public good. . . . Government . . . [can] create jobs directly through . . . development programs." According to this view, government has a moral duty to provide jobs for those left out of the private economy, and the social benefits of intervention outweigh the costs.

During the boom years of the 1990s, the federal government demonstrated a renewed faith in free market principles as the private sector thrived and unemployment levels sank to historic lows. How government should manage the economy to improve the employment prospects of U.S. workers is debated in the following chapter.

"The best way to 'preserve' jobs is to unleash the economy."

Government Intervention Is Not a Solution to Unemployment

David Boaz

In the following viewpoint, David Boaz argues that government intervention in the economy to preserve or create jobs will lead to a misuse of resources, resulting in economic stagnation and a declining standard of living. In Boaz's opinion, unemployment is the short-term side effect of competition as businesses find cheaper means of meeting consumer demands. Economies unrestrained by government intervention will create more new jobs than are lost as a consequence of these market forces, according to the author. Boaz is the executive vice president of the Cato Institute, a libertarian think tank, and the author of *Libertarianism: A Primer.*

As you read, consider the following questions:

1. What lessons, according to Boaz, have Americans learned about the failure of big government?
2. In the author's opinion, what happens when government goes beyond its role of protecting property rights and freedom of exchange?
3. Why does Boaz consider economic policy focused solely on creating jobs "backward"?

The twentieth century has been the century of state power, from Hitler and Stalin to the totalitarian states behind the Iron Curtain, from dictatorships across Africa to the bureaucratic welfare states of North America and Western Europe. Many people assume that as time goes on, and the world becomes more complex, governments naturally get bigger and more powerful. In fact, however, the twentieth century was in many ways a detour from the 2,500-year history of the Western world. From the time of the Greeks, the history of the West has largely been a story of increasing freedom, with a progressively limited role for coercive and arbitrary government.

Learning from Government's Failures

Today, at the end of the twentieth century, there are signs that we may be returning to the path of limiting government and increasing liberty. With the collapse of communism, there is hardly any support left for central planning. Third World countries are privatizing state industries and freeing up markets. Practicing capitalism, the Pacific Rim countries have moved from poverty to world economic leadership in a generation.

In the United States, the bureaucratic leviathan is threatened by a resurgence of the libertarian ideas upon which the country was founded. We are witnessing a breakdown of all the cherished beliefs of the welfare-warfare state. Americans have seen the failure of big government. They learned in the 1960s that governments wage unwinnable wars, spy on their domestic opponents, and lie about it. They learned in the 1970s that government management of the economy leads to inflation, unemployment, and stagnation. They learned in the 1980s that government's cost and intrusiveness grew even as a succession of presidents ran against Washington and promised to change it. Now in the 1990s they are ready to apply those lessons, to make the twenty-first century not the century of the state but the century of the free individual. . . .

Government's Discoordination

What is the role of government in the economy? To begin with, it plays a very important role: protecting property rights and freedom of exchange, so that market prices can bring about coordination of individual plans. When it goes beyond this role, trying to supply particular goods or services or encourage particular outcomes, it not only doesn't help the process of coordination, it actually does the opposite—it *discoordinates*. Prices convey information. If prices are controlled or interfered with by the government, then they won't convey *accurate information*. The more interference, the more inaccurate the information, the less economic coordination, and the less satisfaction of wants. Interference in the information conveyed by prices is just as destructive to

The Folly of Government Job Creation

Contrary to government claims, then, no jobs are "created" when the government embarks on its spending programs to increase employment. These jobs are merely diverted from the recovering private economy. And a job diverted from the private sector to the public sector is invariably a less efficient allocation of resources. This is because production in the private economy is subject to market forces. To survive in the market, the producer must please the consumer, which can be done only by offering a quality product at a good price. . . . And when a consumer receives a product at a lower price, he has money left over to spend on other products—which in turn raises demand, creates jobs, and fosters economic growth.

The public sector, on the other hand, is not subject to market forces. Rather than being profit driven, public works programs are directed by inefficient bureaucrats bound by laws and regulations. Losses in public programs and projects are insignificant in that there are no consequences for the agency incurring the loss. Private sector losses may mean economic ruin for the company and its employees, whereas in the public sector funds appear from the seemingly bottomless well of the public treasury. Thus, the inefficient production of unneeded public goods, although designed to create jobs and stimulate economic growth, in fact has the opposite effect as it drains resources from the recovering private economy, thereby reducing demand, and diverts these funds to the inefficient, unneeded programs and projects. Thus, the intended end is sacrificed to the government's means of achieving it.

Robert Carreira, "The Visible Hand: Government Intervention in the Private Economy," n.d.

economic progress as interference in language would be to having a conversation.

Preserving Jobs

Whenever a better way is found to satisfy any human need (or when demand for any product falls), some of the resources previously employed in satisfying it will no longer be needed. Those no-longer-needed resources may be machines or factories or labor services. Individuals may lose their investments or their jobs when a competitor comes along with a cheaper way of meeting consumers' needs. We should be sympathetic to those who find themselves unemployed or faced with a loss of their investment in such a situation, but we should not lose sight of the *benefits* of competition and creative destruction. People in such a situation often want the government to step in, to maintain demand for their product, or bar a competitor from the market, or somehow preserve their jobs.

In the long run, however, it makes no sense to try to preserve unnecessary jobs or investments. Imagine if we had tried to preserve the jobs in the buggy industry when the automobile came along. We would have been keeping resources— land, labor, and capital—in an industry that could no longer satisfy consumers as well as other uses of those resources. To take a more recent example—one that should be familiar to those who entered school in the 1960s, though perhaps entirely unfamiliar to younger people—the slide rule was completely replaced by the calculator in a matter of just a few years in the 1970s. Should we have preserved the jobs of those making slide rules? For what purpose? Who would have bought slide rules once calculators became available and inexpensive? If we did that every time a firm or an industry became uneconomical, we would soon have a standard of living comparable to that of the Soviet Union.

Efficient Production

It's often said that the point of an economy, or at least of economic policy, is to create jobs. That's backward. The point of an economy is to produce things that people want. If we really wanted to create lots and lots of jobs, the economist

Richard McKenzie points out, we could do it with a three-word federal policy: Outlaw farm machinery. That would create about 60 million jobs, but it would mean withdrawing workers from where they are most productive and using them to produce food that could be produced much more efficiently by fewer workers and more machinery. We would all be much worse off.

Norman Macrae, long-time deputy editor of the *Economist*, has pointed out that in England, since the Industrial Revolution, about two-thirds of all the jobs that existed at the beginning of each century have been eliminated by the end of the century, yet there have been three times as many people employed at the end of the century. He notes that "in the late 1880s, about 60 percent of the work force in both the United States and Britain were in agriculture, domestic service, and jobs related to horse transport. Today, only 3 percent of the work force are in those occupations." During the twentieth century most workers moved from those jobs to manufacturing and then service jobs. During the twenty-first century it's likely that many, perhaps most, workers will move from hands-on production work to information work. Along the way many people will lose their jobs and their investments, but the result will be a higher standard of living for everyone. If we're lucky, fifty years from now we will be producing five times as much output per person as we do today—unless government distorts price signals, impedes coordination, and holds resources in unproductive uses.

In other words, the best way to "preserve" jobs is to unleash the economy. Jobs will *change*, but there will always be more new jobs created than old ones lost. This is true even in cases of technological progress; people get replaced by machines in one field, but the higher level of capital investment in the economy means a rising level of wages for other jobs.

"The public service employment program can eliminate all involuntary unemployment by providing jobs for every person ready, willing, and able to work."

Government Intervention Can Foster Full Employment

Dimitri B. Papadimitriou

Dimitri B. Papadimitriou contends in the following viewpoint that the government should act as the "employer of last resort" by providing public service jobs for every person willing and able to work. Government job creation will lead to full employment by bringing into the labor market the millions of people who remain unemployed even during periods of economic expansion, in Papadimitriou's opinion. According to the author, full employment can be achieved without causing inflation and will counteract the negative effects of unemployment. Papadimitriou is president of the Jerome Levy Economics Institute of Bard College, a public policy research organization.

As you read, consider the following questions:
1. How did William Beveridge define "full employment," according to Papadimitriou?
2. What is the "natural rate of unemployment" and how does it contribute to a "forgotten army" of labor, in the author's opinion?
3. In Papadimitriou's opinion, what are some of the negative effects of unemployment?

Excerpted from "Full Employment Has Not Been Achieved," by Dimitri B. Papadimitriou, *Public Policy Brief*, no. 53, The Jerome Levy Economics Institute, 1999. Reprinted with permission.

Unemployment cannot be conquered by a democracy until it is understood. Full productive employment in a free society is possible but it is not possible without taking pains. It cannot be won by waving a financial wand; it is a goal that can be reached only by conscious continuous organization of all our productive resources under democratic control. To win full employment and keep it, we must will the end and must understand and will the means.

—William Beveridge, 1945

Writing in the 1940s, Beveridge defined full employment as a labor market in which the number of job vacancies is higher than the number of jobless, a condition that guarantees no long-term unemployment. What Beveridge envisaged was achieved in the immediate postwar years, but it was not sustained. However, the U.S. economy now appears to have reached what many believe is "full-employment" with low and stable inflation.

In March 1999 the unemployment rate was announced at 4.2 percent, but unemployment rates as conventionally measured cannot tell the entire story. The job landscape does not seem so rosy when one considers the number of people who are no longer counted as part of the labor force and the number of "employed" who are involuntarily working part-time. The Bureau of Labor Statistics regularly reports large flows in and out of the official categories "unemployed," "employed," and "out of the labor force." In March 1999, for example, of the unemployed, 47.2 percent were job losers, 12.9 percent were job leavers, and 40.0 percent had previously been out of the labor force. People who found jobs typically were new entrants to the labor force or came from the out of the labor force category.

Of the 68 million people in the out of the labor force category, 4.47 million wanted a job, 1.2 million had a marginal attachment to the labor force and were not currently working, and the rest had no attachment to the labor force. In addition, Lester Thurow notes that there are a few million missing males who used to be in the workforce, are not in school, are not old enough to have retired, are neither employed nor unemployed, and are not out of the labor force. They either have dropped out of or have been dropped from the Gross Domestic Product (GDP) machine of the United

States. There are also almost 3.7 million people who are involuntarily working part-time but for statistical purposes are included in the employed category and are not differentiated from those working full-time. Although it is not possible to calculate how many more individuals would work if jobs were made available, these numbers demonstrate that there are undoubtedly millions of these potential workers.

Finally, to make matters worse, the unemployment rate is underestimated if one applies the concept of "disguised" unemployment, defined as employment in sectors with low productivity as compared with productivity in manufacturing. By and large, employment growth has been not in manufacturing but in services, whose productivity lags behind that in manufacturing.

Dismantling Safety Nets

This state of affairs coincides with a rush to embrace deficit reduction in countries throughout the world. Part of the rush to deficit reduction in the United States is a dismantling of the social safety net that has traditionally protected the most vulnerable segments of the population from economic and other hardship. Welfare reform forces recipients off public assistance and leaves it to individual states to find jobs for them, a task the states are unable—even if they are willing—to do. Cutting off aid will not necessarily put people to work. For example, a recent survey in New York State showed that two-thirds of the individuals leaving the rolls of the Aid to Families with Dependent Children (AFDC) and Home Relief programs failed to get jobs. These individuals were left without the means to provide for themselves and their families; the reform forced them deeper into poverty rather than toward self-sufficiency. . . .

During the Great Depression in the United States the government addressed unemployment through direct intervention in the labor market. The government-instituted programs to create jobs were temporary, however, and they were discontinued with the economic recovery that accompanied U.S. entry into World War II. The depression-era and immediate postwar commitment to a "guarantee of employment" was replaced with efforts to "promote maximum employment." In the 1950s and 1960s promotion of full or maximum employment meant macro-economic policies designed to manage aggregate demand, supplemented by selective programs such as job training and limited income maintenance. With the onset of the stagflation of the 1970s, however, even the moderate approach of demand management faltered, and a consensus developed among economists and policymakers worldwide that an unemployment rate of 5 percent in the United States (and as high as 10 percent in France) would be too inflationary.

Rall © Ted Rall. Reprinted with the permission of Universal Press Syndicate. All rights reserved.

The idea of a "natural rate of unemployment," below which unemployment cannot fall without creating inflation, continues to this day. This conventional wisdom requires that to ensure price stability, millions of individuals who are ready, willing, and able to work must remain idle, thereby serving as a "reserve pool" or "forgotten army" of labor. Two important questions, then, may be posed regarding unemployment. First, is the current labor market situation the best we can do in times of prosperity? Second, are we prepared to meet the challenges of the next downturn? (Worrisome signs have already appeared: equity and bond market volatility in the United States and overseas, the Asian and Russian crises, unprecedented rates of household and business indebtedness in the United States, and an obsession with meeting government budget deficit reduction targets everywhere.)

The challenge for policymakers is to craft employment policies that uphold the basic human right to a job and are not inflationary, do not interfere with decisions of individual firms, do not rely on the failed approach of fine-tuning aggregate demand, and are consistent with the fundamental premise that, to the extent possible, socially productive work is preferable to income maintenance. . . .

Public Service Employment

Hyman P. Minsky believed employment policies based on subsidies were liable to lead to inflation, serious financial instability, and financial crisis. He proposed an alternative employment strategy in which government acts as the "employer of last resort." He felt this strategy could promote full employment without the inflationary pressures and structural rigidities usually associated with full employment. A group of researchers at the Levy Institute have developed Minsky's proposals in considerable detail, providing even greater theoretical support for a government job assurance strategy.

The proposal—here called the public service employment program—has two basic components: an employment program that offers workers an opportunity for employment and an exogenously set program wage that protects against inflationary pressures. The first component of the proposal is relatively simple. The government would announce the wage at which it will offer employment to all who want to work and then would employ them at that wage in the public sector. If the government sets the wage at $6.00 per hour, a worker can make $12,500 working full-time, full-year (2,080 hours). Normal public sector employment would not be affected by the plan; it would remain a vital and separate component of public employment. The government would become, in a sense, "a market maker for labor" by establishing a "buffer stock of labor." It would stand ready to "buy" all unemployed labor at a fixed price (wage) or to "sell" it, that is, allow the program labor force to be reduced when the private sector needs labor and offers workers a higher price (wage).

As in all buffer stock schemes, the commodity used as the buffer stock is always fully employed but also available, which means that the program ensures a "loose" labor market even as it ensures full employment. A buffer stock commodity also always has a stable price, which in this case cannot deviate much from the range established by the government's announced wage, so the program ensures stable prices with full employment. . . .

The public service employment program can eliminate all involuntary unemployment by providing jobs for every person ready, willing, and able to work. There will still be many individuals—even among those in the labor force—who will be voluntarily unemployed for a variety of reasons; for example, some may be unwilling to work for the government, others may be unwilling to work for the government's predetermined wage, and still others would prefer to search for a better job. Some individuals will remain unemployed because they cannot meet the minimum standards for public employment. But any person able to work—defined broadly as anyone who can make a contribution to the economy and society, irrespective of the size and type of that contribution— will have the opportunity to do so. . . .

Questions about a program of public service employment (reflecting a variety of political points of view) have been raised. We can respond to some of them briefly.

• *Will the program be another make-work New Deal Works Progress Administration (WPA)?* One way to respond to this question is to cite the many artistic and educational accomplishments and improvements to the nation's physical infrastructure that were the achievements of the WPA. More importantly, the WPA gave to millions of people the opportunity to contribute productively to the American economy and society. Another way to respond is to list the many necessary and beneficial jobs program workers could fill—teachers' aids; library and day care assistants; companions to senior citizens, the bedridden, and the mentally and physically impaired; environmental safety monitors; and many more. The program can provide valuable public services.

• *Can such a program be efficiently administered?* Given the abuses of some public programs, concerns about administering the program are legitimate. However, there have also been some model programs, such as Volunteers in Service to America (VISTA), the Peace Corps, and Americorps.

• *Since states are already implementing welfare-to-work programs, why is this program needed?* With only a few exceptions, states have indicated that they will not offer permanent work to former welfare recipients. They will be left to fend for themselves.

• *Will a stigma be attached to participation in such a program?* Peace Corps, VISTA, and Americorps participants have been well regarded. A public service work assignment may prove to be a good entry on a resume.

• *Why worry now, when unemployment is at its lowest level in a generation?* A closer look at the official unemployment statistics shows that the country is not a "worker heaven." The large population of involuntarily unemployed and underemployed warrants concern in a country that considers socially productive work a virtue and upholds the right of its citizens to employment.

A Cost-Effective Solution to Unemployment

It is difficult to see how truly full employment under a public service job opportunity program could be more inflationary than our current system of maintaining a reserve army of the unemployed and public assistance, a system that pays people for not working, allows their human capital to depreciate, and results in the high economic and social costs associated with unemployment. Wage subsidies and reductions in the workweek, even if they turn out to be successful at increasing employment substantially, could result in the inflation and sluggish growth associated with tight labor markets and structural rigidities. In contrast, a public service employment solution provides full employment with price stability and labor market flexibility. As Minsky put it, "only an infinitely elastic demand for labor can guarantee full employment without setting off a wage-price spiral, and only government can create an infinitely elastic demand for labor." At the same time, as long as those holding a program job are available when private sector demand increases, such a program will not result in inflationary pressures or structural rigidities. The public service employment approach also will be relatively inexpensive and likely to pay for itself. It can preserve human capital and provide valuable public services.

The costs of unemployment are significant and many of them can be quantified, especially those associated with the loss of output that unemployed workers could have produced. Furthermore, the employed (and their employers) are burdened with financing the unemployment insurance and other maintenance support the unemployed receive. Alas, the "damages" of unemployment do not stop there. Negative effects that afflict the unemployed include loss of freedom and social exclusion, poor health, discouragement and loss of motivation for future work, weakening of family structure, cynicism and ultimate loss of social values and self-reliance, and psychological suffering even to the point of suicide. Unemployment also breeds racial and gender intolerance. It engenders resistance to organizational flexibility and promotes technical conservatism in those currently employed who fear downsizing and joblessness. . . .

In the United States the government has gradually retreated from Franklin Roosevelt's assertion of everyone's "right to employment" and the initial push to "guarantee full employment." The Employment Act of 1946 reduced the commitment to the "promotion" of "maximum employment," and since the 1970s the commitment has been reduced still further to the acceptance of a rather large "natural rate of unemployment." But the real issue is . . . to work toward making policy-makers willing to learn from the successful (and failed) policies of the past, amend them to reflect current economic conditions, and, finally, marshal the needed resources to implement them. . . .

Should progress toward genuinely full employment be today's task for economists? I think so. I hope so. As Beveridge said, "To win full employment and keep it, we must will the end and understand and will the means."

"Welfare reformers were correct to predict that most welfare recipients could provide for themselves and their children."

Welfare-to-Work Programs Help Disadvantaged Workers

Ron Haskins

In 1996, the federal welfare program was replaced with Temporary Aid to Needy Families, a welfare-to-work program that requires recipients to find work within a certain time period or lose their benefits. Ron Haskins contends in the following viewpoint that welfare-to-work programs, with their emphasis on "work first," have been highly successful, resulting in unprecedented declines in welfare rolls from coast to coast. In addition, the employment and income rates of female-headed households have increased while their poverty rates have dropped, according to the author. Haskins is the staff director of the Human Resources Subcommittee of the U.S. House Ways and Means Committee.

As you read, consider the following questions:
1. In the author's opinion, how do welfare-to-work programs differ from the previous welfare system's approach to job training?
2. By what percentage have national welfare rolls shrunk since their peak in March 1994, according to Haskins?
3. What accounts for the success of welfare-to-work programs, in Haskins's opinion?

Reprinted, with permission, from "Welfare Reform Is Working," by Ron Haskins, *The American Enterprise*, January 1999. Copyright © 1999 by the American Enterprise Institute for Public Policy Research.

As I drove up Interstate 5 from San Diego to Long Beach, I thought back over 20-plus years of visiting welfare offices. Drab operations they were—interviewing moms, filling out 20-page forms, seeking verification of assets and income, calculating benefit amounts, all to spit out the grand product: government checks.

Since the passage of welfare reform in 1996, reports have suggested that a lot is changing in the way states administer welfare. But nothing prepared me for what I was about to witness.

As I pulled into the parking lot of the Regional Work Center in Long Beach, I was greeted by a young man in a blue blazer who ushered me into a large room with 15 people. For the next two hours, I heard a lot about jobs, training, wages, transportation, and child care. But nothing, absolutely nothing, about benefit levels or check writing.

The most striking thing about the meeting was the participants. In addition to the welfare administrators and recipients—standard fare for such meetings—we were joined by the president of Franklin Brass, an assembly and packaging company with about 400 employees; a regional personnel manager for United Airlines; the director of development for Delco Machine and Gear, a small machine company with about 90 employees; and the chief hiring agent for the Volt Company, a temporary employment agency. All were on a first-name basis with the administrator who ran the work program, Frank Mora. Each of the employers told me about their involvement with the program and then introduced one of the former welfare recipients they had hired. The work program administrators jumped in occasionally to explain various details of coordination or to propound their work-first philosophy.

Here's a typical story. Jim was a 19-year-old with two children, a wife, no job, and little education. When he and his wife applied for welfare benefits, Mora gave him an appointment to help him find a job. After Jim missed the appointment, Mora went to his apartment to find out why. Jim lived in a gang-infested neighborhood and had stayed home with a sick child. Mora gave him another appointment, worked with Jim and the local housing authority to find him a better apartment in a better neighborhood, and got him an interview with Delco. After several months on the job, the company was so impressed with Jim they offered to help pay for extensive training as a machine operator. When he finishes the training, Jim will be earning over $15 per hour with benefits.

Under the old welfare regime, education and training programs for welfare recipients were often used by administrators as diversionary tactics to avoid actual work. By contrast, consider this example of training under the new regime: In his conversations with employers and his reading of want ads, Mora noticed lots of local demand for forklift operators. So he worked with officials at Long Beach City College to design a four-day course in forklift operation. In the first year, about 1,200 adults applying for or receiving welfare completed the course. Mora reports that 90 percent of them are now employed operating forklifts and earning at least $8 per hour with benefits. . . .

Like the Long Beach office, welfare offices all over Los Angeles County are transforming themselves into job-placement centers. The result is that welfare rolls are dropping precipitously. Over a 10-month period between 1997–98, the rolls in Los Angeles dropped more than 100,000, saving the state $54 million each month. Counties in the rest of California, including those with double-digit unemployment, report similar declines. According to the state's principal economist, it's "the only extended caseload reduction we have ever had."

Switch coasts. We are now headed to the Anne Arundel County Job Center in Annapolis, Maryland, accompanied by a small delegation of British visitors intent on learning about American welfare reform. The British delegation is headed by Keith Bradley, Undersecretary for Social Welfare in the House of Commons.

We're visiting a program run by Democrats in a state controlled by Democrats, which is nice if you're a member of the British Labour party. Surely here we will find the old entitlement mentality and hostility toward the idea of replacing welfare with work.

On the way to the conference room, however, we pass walls decorated with posters touting the benefits of work and press accounts of former welfare mothers who've left welfare for jobs. As potential welfare dependents talk with job counselors in this converted bank building, a quiet efficiency pervades the place.

Reform in Wisconsin

Wisconsin was a pioneer, beginning its program a decade before the 1996 law was passed. By January 1997 Wisconsin had already reduced its welfare caseload by 54 percent from what it was in January 1987. The state, which had been sending out $46 million of welfare checks a month in 1987, had reduced that amount to $21 million a month. Answering the claim that welfare caseloads only decline during good times, the Wisconsin decline occurred during the recession of the early 1990s.

What happened in Wisconsin? "Welfare reform in Wisconsin began with one simple premise: Every person is capable of doing something," Gov. Tommy Thompson has said. Accordingly, the state used four different approaches, depending on the welfare recipient's ability to work.

• Those considered ready for a job were placed in an unsubsidized job, usually in the private sector.

• Those with no work history were placed in a subsidized job for six to nine months.

• Those who didn't have necessary skills and work habits were placed in a community-service job for six to nine months to learn what was needed.

• Those who couldn't even do community work were required to participate in whatever activities they were able to do. . . .

At the beginning of 1985, the welfare caseload in Wisconsin was 94,778. By the end of 1998, it was 10,185—an 89.3 percent reduction.

Pete Du Pont, *World and I*, January 2000.

In the course of an hour's discussion, we hear more or less the same things the program managers said in Long Beach. Again, no talk about benefits; instead, all the talk is about job placements, child care, transportation, training. The enthusiasm in this office is electric. The attitude of the staff is, We should have been doing this all along.

And what "this" is can be stated simply: helping welfare applicants get a job before they get welfare. The first thing you see on the wall of the Annapolis office are the words "Job

Center"—"welfare" is nowhere to be found. And they're not kidding. In a typical month, 1,700 "customers" walk into the Job Center. Fewer than 100 (6 percent) will wind up on cash welfare. The rest are diverted, mostly to employment.

Before the customers can even ask for cash welfare, they are interviewed by a job counselor who believes they can and should work. Then they are helped to prepare a resume on the Center's public computer, assisted in arranging job interviews (using the phone bank available in the Job Center), provided with on-site child care if necessary, told about available education and training courses (which are not allowed to interfere with getting a job), and signed up for child support. The Job Center even has clothes available so the customers can dress properly for interviews. And if the customer has a transportation problem in this rural county with little public transportation, the job counselor is likely to sign her up for the lease-to-purchase plan for discarded county vehicles.

As in Los Angeles, data on the Annapolis program are clear and consistent. That only 6 percent of the adults who come into the Job Center in a typical month wind up on welfare indicates that this is a completely new kind of "welfare" program. And even among those who actually apply for welfare, only half receive cash benefits before they get a job.

Here are two more striking statistics. In October 1996, when the program started, the county spent $830,000 per month on cash welfare. A year later, the county spent $680,000, a 20 percent reduction. When the county started the Job Center, 9,100 families drew cash welfare. A year later the rolls had plummeted by 40 percent.

Welfare declines like these are completely without historical precedent—but nowadays they are routine. The national rolls have shrunk by an astonishing 40 percent since their peak in March 1994. The highest previous decline in cash welfare rolls over any period of two or more years was 8 percent.

Lest anyone conclude that the current economic boom explains the decline, consider the Reagan expansion that began in 1982. As the economy added 17 million jobs over eight years, the welfare caseload actually increased by 13 percent.

Even during the first three years of the current expansion, the welfare caseload expanded even as national employment grew. It was not until 1994, with the states implementing their own partial welfare reforms under Reagan-Bush waivers from federal rules, that the welfare caseload began to decline. Then, after the Republican Congress passed federal reform in 1996, caseloads plummeted. They are now dropping at the rate of nearly 6,000 recipients per day.

Caseload declines are an important indicator of success because they are an indirect measure of welfare families achieving self-reliance. But female employment and earnings are even more important indicators of success, and evidence is accumulating that welfare reform has had major effects on both. The Bureau of Labor Statistics reports that after cruising along at about 136,000 per year, the net increase in single-mothers with jobs rose to 272,000, a figure higher than ever before, in the 12-month period ending in October 1996—just as the states were implementing reforms on a limited basis. Over the next 12 months, after every state had implemented the federal welfare reform law, the figure exploded to 456,000.

As reform began to drive welfare rolls down, the rate of employment among never-married, separated, and divorced mothers with children—precisely the mothers most likely to be on welfare—rose significantly, according to recent studies. John Bishop of Cornell, for example, reports that the percentage of never-married mothers holding jobs jumped an unprecedented 32 percent from 1994–98. By contrast, the rate of work among these mothers had been virtually flat for the previous 15 years. Over this same four-year period (a time of labor shortages in much of the country), fully two-thirds of all increases in U.S. workforce participation were attributable to welfare reform and increases in the federal tax credit for low-income workers.

There is also evidence, from New Jersey and elsewhere, that welfare reforms have helped reduce out-of-wedlock births among welfare mothers. If a better work ethic among unmarried mothers is now combining with reduced illegitimacy, leaving fewer children to grow up without a father in the first place, then some truly profound improvements in American social life will follow. And there are indications this is beginning to happen.

The dramatic decline in welfare rolls has not produced the increase in poverty that was widely predicted by opponents of welfare reform. In 1997, the Census Bureau has just reported, children's poverty declined for the fourth year in a row, and the rate for black children declined by the largest single-year amount ever, to the lowest rate on record in the U.S. The poverty rate for black female-headed families with children declined by a remarkable 4.1 percentage points, also by far the greatest decline ever.

Liberal opponents of welfare reform predicted that mothers pushed from public assistance to low-wage jobs would experience substantial declines in their incomes as a result. Now that lots of mothers have made the move, what does the evidence show? An analysis prepared by the [former] Clinton administration's Office of Management and Budget found that single mothers living in the poorest 40 percent of U.S. households received a total of $4 billion less in welfare income in 1997 than in 1993 (after taking inflation into account). But their earned income increased by $4.3 billion, and they also received another $2.1 billion increase from the earned income tax credit. Adding up all their sources of income, the nation's poorest mothers had nearly $3.8 billion more in 1997 than 1993. So much for income declines. More importantly, they made their money the old-fashioned way. Next thing you know, they'll be investing.

So while welfare rolls were plummeting, the employment rates of female-headed families soared, their poverty rates dropped, and their income increased. At the same time, the national illegitimacy trends reversed. This happy portrait, based on highly reliable national data, has no precedent in U.S. social history.

Given the modest success or outright failure of most social reforms attempted by government, what accounts for the impressive success of welfare reform? In the next several years, we will be treated to torturous explanations from social scientists. The real answer, though, is quite simple: As long as welfare was an entitlement, with opinion leaders and social workers telling people they had an inalienable right to unlimited benefits, more and more people signed up and stayed for longer and longer spells. By the mid-1980s, the average duration on welfare for families on the rolls at a given moment was an amazing 13 years. In short, millions of young mothers were victims of what psychologists call "learned helplessness."

But then reformers in Congress, joined by the [former] Clinton administration, pushed through a tough set of changes designed to end welfare as a vocation. The essence of their plan was, first, to require persons on welfare to work, beginning the first day they walk through the door seeking benefits. Social workers trying to wrap cocoons of entitlements around able-bodied young Americans had to be converted into social workers who would tell applicants they should, can, and must provide for themselves. Second, firm time limits were placed on benefits, to signal that welfare is an aberration and self-reliance normal. Third, states were given authority to impose sanctions, including the cessation of all cash benefits, on adults not willing to work. Finally, federal entitlements that blindly paid money directly to individuals were converted into block grants to state governments set at a fixed amount. This change gave state and local governments a financial incentive to help people get off welfare. Under the old entitlement system, if states reduced their caseloads, the federal government "rewarded" them by cutting their federal dollars. Now, if states reduce their caseloads, they retain all the savings.

Although liberals in Congress, academia, and the media rarely said so explicitly, they assumed that adults on welfare were incapable of supporting themselves and therefore needed a protective blanket of federal entitlements. Studies will soon provide more detail on why people are leaving welfare at today's unprecedented rates, but we already know enough to conclude that the majority leave because they find work, and most of the rest either were already working or have other means of support. Welfare reformers were correct to predict that most welfare recipients could provide for themselves and their children.

The Benefits of Employment

The confidence reformers placed in state and local governments is also paying off. Instead of the slashed benefits and "race to the bottom" predicted by opponents of reform, states are mounting scores of innovative programs. Virtually every state now has offices like those in Long Beach and Annapolis that help low-income families make the transition from welfare to work—or avoid welfare altogether. And states are using the money they save from reduced caseloads to pay for work-promoting services such as child care and transportation, helping former recipients keep their jobs and, in some cases, get the education and training they need for better jobs.

It needs to be remembered that many of the mothers avoiding welfare today receive public subsidies of $5,000 or more even after they leave welfare (providing medical, food, or child care benefits, for instance). Critics may object to these benefits as little more than welfare by a different name. But most Americans believe it is better for adults to be productively employed than idle and dependent, and adults who can command only low wages will not leave welfare until they can actually support themselves and their children.

Starting in the 1980s, Democrats and Republicans began developing a system of non-cash benefits, contingent on work, that makes low-wage jobs economically attractive for mothers with children. Once this system was in place, the 1996 welfare reforms forced welfare-dependent mothers into self-reliance—and the pleasant discovery that they had more money and benefits (not to mention a better feeling about themselves and their place in society) when they were working, even in low-wage jobs.

The nation is now well along in creating a balanced system of public benefits that combines carrots and sticks. This success is producing a social revolution whose beneficial effects on American society are just beginning to emerge. If the nation holds steady on this course—and especially if Congress expands the new requirements to other welfare and unemployment programs—low-skilled parents, their children, and American taxpayers will all be better off.

> *"Research on the effects of welfare reform*
> *suggest that its main effect so far has been*
> *to increase the ranks of the working poor."*

Welfare-to-Work Programs Harm the Disadvantaged

Randy Albelda

In the following viewpoint, Randy Albelda argues that welfare-to-work programs, introduced under a 1996 welfare reform law, have reduced welfare rolls at the expense of single mothers, who must now accept low-paying menial jobs or lose their benefits. Welfare-to-work programs discourage training and have failed to address the needs of struggling families or move former recipients out of poverty, in the author's opinion. Albelda is a professor of economics at the University of Massachusetts, Boston.

As you read, consider the following questions:
1. Under federal time limits, how many years can families receive welfare assistance, according to Albelda?
2. How did former welfare recipients in South Carolina respond when surveyed about their post-welfare lives, as reported by the author?
3. What did researchers conclude about the monthly earnings of former welfare recipients, according to the author?

From "What Welfare Reform Has Wrought," by Randy Albelda, *Dollars & Sense*, January/February 1999. Reprinted by permission of *Dollars & Sense*, a progressive economics magazine; www.dollarsandsense.org.

E nding "welfare as we know it" was just a campaign slogan for Bill Clinton in 1992, but its human effects are now being felt. Consider "Fern," a single mother in Connecticut with children ages twelve, five, and four. Under the old welfare law, Fern was attending school almost full-time, trying to get a B.A., and getting by on welfare, food stamps, and child care assistance. But under welfare reform, as of November 1997 Fern had to quit school or risk being "sanctioned" and losing her food stamps and child care, reports the Welfare and Human Rights Monitoring Project of the Unitarian Universalist Service Committee (UUSC).

A California woman named "Joyce," whose children are ages one and three, told the UUSC: "I took a terrible job because my [social] worker told me if I didn't he would cut me off benefits. I have been sexually harassed at this job and I told the worker about this. I told him I could not keep dealing with this kind of thing. He said it was my decision. I could quit and lose my benefits or keep the job."

Complying with the New Rules

Those wondering why the public assistance rolls have dropped drastically over the last five years should talk to Fern and Joyce before celebrating the success of state and federal welfare reform. Congress and [former President] Clinton abolished the welfare program AFDC (Aid to Families with Dependent Children) in August 1996 and replaced it with Temporary Aid to Needy Families (TANF), which requires people receiving assistance to find employment or be placed in unpaid jobs for 20 hours a week or more as quickly as possible. Long term training and education are discouraged and in some states are virtually prohibited. Over 80% of the states also reformed their systems over the last decade and many have stricter requirements than those imposed by TANF.

Families are sanctioned—meaning they lose all or part of their assistance—if they do not comply with welfare rules, which are plentiful. And, perhaps most important, TANF caps a parent's assistance at five years during their lifetime. All but three states have set their own time limits, ranging from as little as 21 months to the 60 month federal limit.

Research on the effects of welfare reform suggest that its main effect so far has been to increase the ranks of the working poor. And as bad as that might be, it's actually worse than it sounds. That's because the new working poor are mostly single mothers, laboring at paid jobs for large chunks of the day, while also raising young children. This brings a whole new meaning to the tradeoff between paid work and caring for one's family.

Prior to TANF, when any state changed its welfare provisions, the state was required by law to evaluate the impact. The resulting studies provided little, if any, evidence that the new emphasis on work by the feds and most states will alleviate poverty or the need for welfare. This helps explain why the 1996 law focuses on time limits—since "reform" cannot eliminate the need for welfare, the only way to keep people from returning to the rolls is to ban them from receiving assistance.

Researchers found that short-term employment programs caused women to leave welfare quicker, but they returned at the same rates as before, and increased their earnings only slightly compared to women who also received welfare but did not participate in work requirements. Women who engaged in longer-term education and employment programs earned more, for more time, than those in the traditional welfare program. They tended to stay on welfare longer (since their education and training took longer), but had slightly lower return rates.

TANF: Less Welfare, Just as Much Poverty

With the passage of TANF, poverty researchers and liberal foundations got very nervous. Few had anticipated such sweeping reforms, and the law did not require evaluations of the new welfare rules. As a result, foundations, independent researchers, university and policy centers, and states have launched a whole host of welfare-related research. While many of the findings have not yet been published, the results are beginning to paint a clear picture.

In February 1998, the National Conference of State Legislatures (NCSL) summarized the results of studies completed in nine states that look at people who have left the welfare roles. Some people leave because they are sanctioned, some because they earn too much and are no longer eligible, and others because they no longer want to receive assistance. The NCSL concluded that while most former recipients are finding employment, most are not earning enough to bring their families out of poverty.

One study, in South Carolina, surveyed more than 500 adult former welfare recipients. Three out of every five were employed, working an average of 34 hours a week, and making $6.34 an hour. Of those not working, 20% said they couldn't find a job, another 17% reported lack of child care, 15% had an injury or illness, and 12% lacked transportation. Perhaps it was a great victory for reform that 60% of welfare moms had found jobs?

Not really, because their lives had, if anything, gotten worse. When asked about providing for their families while off welfare versus on it, 50% said they currently were behind in paying their rent or utilities—versus 39% when they were on welfare; 14% now could not pay for medical care versus 3% while on welfare; and 16% said they now had periods without enough money to buy food, versus 7% while on welfare.

A forthcoming report by Sharon Parrott for the Center on Budget and Policy Priorities summarizes studies of former welfare recipients in 12 states. Analyses in Indiana, Maryland, South Carolina, Ohio, and Wisconsin found that between one-half and two-thirds of parents were employed soon after leaving the welfare rolls, regardless of why they left. In Florida, Indiana, Minnesota, Oregon, and Washington state, researchers found that most former recipients are nearly fully engaged in the paid labor force and work 30 hours or more a week when they are employed.

Below-Poverty Wages

Those who argue that welfare reform is a success point to the large number of mothers who now have paid jobs. What they don't like to tell us is that mothers and their children are still poor. In Pensacola, Florida, for example, three-quarters of former and current recipients with earnings made less than $7.00 an hour; the average wage for city dwellers who had been on welfare for many years in Minnesota was $6.55 an hour; recipients who found jobs averaged $7.34 an hour in Portland, Oregon; and former working recipients averaged $6.44 in South Carolina. Not nearly enough to support a family.

Monthly Earnings of Welfare Recipients* Who Find Employment

Area Studied	Monthly Earnings	As a Percent of Federal Poverty Line
Los Angeles	$695	67%
Delaware	$705	66%
Escambia County, Florida	$682	65%
Michigan	$907	90%
Minnesota (five urban counties)	$699	67%
Portland, Oregon	$712	70%

* Including those no longer receiving assistance and those combining welfare and work

Note: The types of families included and time periods involved varied between the geographic areas. Years are 1996 and/or 1997 except for Portland, which was 1993 to 1994.

Sharon Parrott, "Welfare Recipients Who Find Jobs: What Do We Know About Their Employment and Earnings?" Center on Budget and Policy Priorities, November 16, 1998.

When researchers looked at total earnings received over several months (rather than their hourly wages), they found that most fell well below the poverty level. In Milwaukee, 75% of former recipients had earnings below the poverty line. In Maryland, the average earnings amounted to $9,500 a year. Researchers in Delaware, Minnesota, and Oregon, and in the cities of Los Angeles and Pensacola, Florida found that the earnings of current participants in states' work demonstration programs averaged two-thirds of the official poverty line.

These earnings levels come as no surprise when you look at the kinds of jobs recipients find. More than one-third of former recipients in Maryland were working in wholesale or retail trade. Almost half of those in South Carolina were in service occupations, mostly at food preparation, temp work, or in hotels and motels. Close to one-third of the employed former recipients in Milwaukee found jobs through temp agencies.

Work Before Family

And there is no such thing as "family-friendly" policies at the workplaces of recipients who are supporting their families. In the four states that researchers checked, only 40% to 60% of employers offered health insurance. Two of the studies asked about vacation time and sick leave policies: only about one-third of employees were eligible for sick days and less than half received paid vacation time. A sick kid can often translate into a missed day of work and lower earnings, and several sick days can often result in losing a job.

Note that the findings reported here are only for those who did find jobs. Over one-third of women who leave welfare are not showing up in employment records, and much less is known about them. Many have moved out of the state which was conducting the study. Many others may have found a partner or moved in with family members or a boyfriend—situations that could be dangerous or undesirable. And while food pantries and homeless shelters are reporting increased use, we don't yet know how many women and their children are subsisting in horrible conditions, without adequate food, shelter, clothing, or medical care.

"Comprehensive federal legislation can secure a realistic living wage for all workers."

A National Living Wage Will Improve Living Standards

Committees of Correspondence for Democracy and Socialism

The Committees of Correspondence for Democracy and Socialism (CoC) is an organization working to find solutions to the problems of poverty and unemployment in the United States. In the following viewpoint, the CoC argues that the federal minimum hourly wage should be determined by a formula that allows a full-time worker's earnings to provide for the basic needs of a family of four. Replacing the inadequate minimum wage with a living wage formula will raise the living standards of the millions of U.S. workers with jobs paying wages at or below the federal poverty level, according to the CoC.

As you read, consider the following questions:
1. What percentage of the nation's wealth is controlled by the most affluent 1 percent, according to the CoC?
2. In the authors' opinion, what hourly wage is needed to keep a family above the poverty level?
3. Aside from the living wage formula, what other amendments does the CoC propose to the 1938 Fair Standards Labor Law?

Excerpted from "Urgent: A Living Wage for Everyone Who Works," by the Committees of Correspondence for Democracy and Socialism, February 2000. Reprinted with permission. For more information please contact CCDS at NATCOFC@aol.com; www.cofc.org; fax: (212) 233-7063; telephone: (212) 233-7151.

M illions of people in our country work at low wage jobs that keep them in grinding poverty. Some full time workers are paid wages so low the family must live in a public shelter. Women and men in low wage jobs are the fastest growing sector of the workforce.

The Living Wage Movement

In response, working people and their allies have been organizing to end this abuse and assure an income adequate to sustain a family. The living wage idea has emerged in scores of communities around the country to counter the free wheeling capitalism that has devastated the lives of so many. A living wage movement of growing strength and potential has come into being, which has already won limited victories in 40 municipalities. This is a historic movement, which gives hope that the negative trend in living standards for so many can be reversed. Immigrant rights organizations, trade unions, tenant and housing groups and the whole country will benefit from victories in the campaign for a living wage.

The idea we put forward here for consideration is that only comprehensive federal legislation can secure a realistic living wage for all workers. It will take a powerful coalition of many forces, communities and organizations, building on the existing movement, to make this a reality.

We would like to celebrate the new millennium by starting to build that coalition now. Our basic proposal is an amendment to the Minimum Wage Act of 1938, which is further elaborated in the following pages.

Good Times Are Not for Everyone

Every day headlines blare that good times are rolling. But you have to get to the fine print to learn that the "good times" are not for everyone. Not by a long shot.

We live in a country where the growing gap between rich and poor has become incredibly obscene and hurtful. The richest 2.7 million people have as much income as the poorest 100 million. The most affluent 1% control 40% of the nation's wealth. The Congressional Budget Office reports income disparity between rich and poor keeps growing. The bottom 80% of all U.S. households are now taking home

50% of the national income, down from 56% in 1977. Despite slight gains in the average worker's income in 1999, income inequality is at its highest level since the Census Bureau began tracking it. Working people are losing ground dangerously in the battle for a decent slice of the economic pie.

In the richest country of the world, where 12,000 Americans reported income of a million dollars or more in 1997, the average income of the poorest 20% of households is estimated at $8800 for 1999, even less than they earned 20 years ago. By contrast, the U.S. Department of Health and Human Services now sets the poverty level for a family of four at a minimal annual income of $17,000, about $8.50 an hour.

Why such a growing gap between rich and poor in the world's wealthiest nation? Why this chasm when there are sufficient resources to provide everyone with adequate food, housing, clothing, education, medical care and a good standard of living? At a time when the bull market rewards investors, brokers and CEO's with unprecedented riches, the U.S. Conference of Mayors reports that emergency food requests jumped 16% from 1996 to 1997 and that the leading cause of hunger was wages that are at poverty level or below. At last count, at least one family member was working in 40% of all families seeking emergency food aid.

"Flipper Jobs" and Declining Incomes

The Dow Jones may be soaring, but John and Mary Jones are in a dangerous slump. In 1998, nearly 1 in 3 U.S. workers had jobs paying at or below the federal poverty level, says the Bureau of Labor Statistics. "Flipper jobs", hamburger flippers, mattress flippers, symbolize our economy. Poverty level, low wage jobs for full time workers in restaurants, motels, hospitals, stores, public buildings and other services are an increasing proportion of the total job market. The Economics Policy Institute (EPI) says that 28.5 million workers earn less than $8.00 an hour, and a total of 44.2 million, or 40% of all workers (aged 18–64) earn wages that bring an income below the latest poverty level. Between 1973 and 1997 only the top 20% of all workers had an increase, in real dollar terms. The real income of the remaining 80% declined.

In the U.S., with its deeply rooted racism, the situation of people of colors is worst of all. In 1997, 38% of all African American workers earned poverty wages, up from 33% in 1979. Forty-seven percent of Latino workers earned poverty wages in 1997, up from 34% in 1979. The small improvement in 1999 wages in communities of color came about because these communities benefited most from the increase in the minimum wage. But unemployment rates continue to be higher in Latino and African-American communities and the wage levels are still considerably lower than those of the general population.

The minimum wage is considered a safety net, assuring workers an income able to sustain a family. The numbers, however, expose the hollowness of that claim.

Struggling on the Current Minimum Wage

Inflation has eroded the real purchasing power of the minimum wage and its real value has declined since the late 1960's. As calculated by EPI, "the value of the minimum wage in 1997 was 18.1% less than in 1970." Senator Barbara Boxer of California says, "About 760,000 Southern California workers earn the state's minimum wage, which is now $5.75 an hour—less than $12,000 a year. The purchasing power of this wage is about $2 an hour lower than the purchasing power of the minimum wage in 1968."

While $8.50 an hour is needed to keep a family above the poverty level, Congress hassles and grouses over a law which brings the minimum wage to $6.15 in three years. Establishing a minimum wage was a major victory for working people and pressure on Congress must be unrelenting to pass laws supportive of low-income workers. But the minimum wage as now conceived and legislated is not the road out of poverty. It condemns minimum wage workers, and those whose wage is slightly above the minimum— about 20% of the work force, and their families—to a needy and demeaning existence.

Higher Wages and Benefits for All

The widespread demand for a living wage is one way working people have responded to this outrage. In 40 cities and counties in 17 states U.S. workers have won living wage ordinances. A living wage movement, formed by community organizations, religious groups, trade unions and others, has won a place for itself on the national scene. As the struggle has evolved from area to area, the trend has been to escalate the dollar demands and improve the benefit provisions like health insurance, sick pay and the right to form unions. Madeline Janis-Aparicio, director of the Los Angeles Living Wage Coalition says, "You have to look at the living wage movement in the context of the utter failure of federal labor law, now so stacked against workers." It is estimated that more than 50 additional cities and counties are now considering living wage legislation.

"IF WE PAY THEM STARVATION WAGES, WHY DO THEY NEED A LUNCH BREAK?"

© Carol Simpson Productions. Used with permission.

A limitation of this very significant development is that *the living wage victories apply to so few.* While bringing real benefits to the workers covered, the ordinances affect only employees of companies with city contracts, or get city tax breaks. This comes to a tiny portion of the working population. When enacted in Los Angeles, for example, it affected 7600 workers, or 3/10 of 1% of the local work force. Nationwide living wage ordinances cover about 44,000 workers, researchers Robert Pollin, Stephanie Luce and Mark Brenner calculate. As Rev. Martin Luther King proposed more than 30 years ago, we need to raise the minimum wage to the level of a living wage that will keep working families out of poverty. *We need a living wage for everyone who works!*

While profits skyrocket, most working people cannot even hold their own in this market-driven economy. If this goes unchallenged, living standards of the working majority will continue to plunge while a handful continue to accumulate unimaginable wealth. *Only comprehensive federal legislation can begin to address this situation.*

The Committees of Correspondence for Democracy and Socialism has a proposal to the Living Wage movement that would extend the movement's reach and give it true national scope. We urge passage of a federal law making a realistic living wage the minimum wage. Moreover the law, to be meaningful, must provide for medical care and childcare.

A Standard of Fairness for the New Century

When Congress passed the Fair Labor Standards Act in 1938 (the minimum wage law) it outlawed "labor conditions detrimental to the maintenance of the minimum standard of living necessary for health, efficiency and general well-being of workers." That law guaranteed a minimum hourly wage, set the standard 40-hour workweek, and prohibited child labor and sex discrimination in wages.

Conditions have changed in the last 60 years. Today working people are in a desperate battle to keep gains they have won over the years from being eroded. Low income jobs which force people to choose between buying food or medicine fit precisely "conditions detrimental to the maintenance of a minimum standard of living" proscribed in the 1938 law. The great increase in the number of two-parent and single-parent families where all parents are wage earners means that access to quality child care from early infancy should be regarded as a fundamental labor concern. Until single payer national health coverage is won, the 44 million without health insurance underscore the urgent need to require employer financed health care. It is time to amend and extend the benefits of the 1938 Fair Standards Labor Law.

Our legislative proposal would amend the law as follows:

(1) the minimum hourly wage to be fixed by a formula that

allows a full time worker's earnings to provide the most basic personal consumption needs of a family of four.

(2) Congress would be directed to extend the Medicare program so that every working family can be fully covered from the first day of employment to the end of the period covered by unemployment insurance.

(3) Congress would be directed to expand the Head Start program to provide childcare accessible to every working family in a safe and developmentally appropriate environment.

Challenging the Drive to Maximize Profits

The formula we propose to determine the minimum wage is similar to that used by many non-profit organizations to arrive at a basic wage level required for a family's economic self-sufficiency. A wage between $10 and $12 per hour would be considered a reasonable expectation today. It would promote security in the entire economy by raising payrolls. The increase in payroll tax revenues would strengthen the Social Security system and talk of privatizing it could be laid to rest. The development of health care and child care industries, as proposed in the legislative draft, would create more living wage jobs that would be insulated against world economic crises.

We understand the depth and gravity of the campaign we are proposing. It is a challenge to the inherent capitalist drive to maximize profits for the major owners of capital no matter what misery it may create for millions in our country, and billions in the world. We know the profiteers who benefit from the present order of things will place all kinds of hurdles and obstacles and create major problems to obstruct and prevent the achievement of so momentous a change. In taking this initiative we have no illusions about the difficulties and struggles ahead, or the magnitude of the task. It will be a very long and hard fight to win a greater measure of economic justice.

The main beneficiaries of the campaign for a living wage for all would be women, people of color, immigrants, disabled workers and the lowest paid workers in the country and their families. It is a campaign to close the wage gap based on racism, sexism and discrimination against seniors and youth.

Raising wages of the lowest paid will also have an uplifting effect on all wages. The battle for a living wage will boost union organizing and should be combined with it. The unorganized are in urgent need of union protection, and they are ready to enter the fold, as the successful Justice for Janitors and nursing home and home care workers campaigns show. It is a good and hopeful sign that the American Federation of Labor-Congress of Industrial Organizations (AFL-CIO) unions are now more actively organizing low-paid and, often, immigrant workers. The organized labor movement cannot expand and progress without taking in this growing sector.

The fight for passage of the bill cannot be successful without strong trade union participation. Organized labor should be a major player in the struggle to win back gains yielded in the Reagan years. A living wage law is the best way to generate an upward push on all wages, to defend all working people from the ongoing attack on our living standards.

Experience has shown that this can be an inclusive movement fighting for a decent life for everyone. Many community, religious and other organizations, as well as trade unions have joined forces to forge the victories already won. In Baltimore, the living wage campaign was initiated by a coalition of the American Federation of State, County, and Municipal Employees (AFSCME) and about 50 churches of various denominations. The living wage campaign in Chicago brought together community groups like the Northwest Neighborhood Federation, many trade unions, 7 elected officials, religious organizations and activist groups. In virtually every successful campaign, an active coalition carried the burden of outreach, organizing street heat and relations with elected bodies to see the project through.

Putting Pressure on Congress

We propose a Congressional bill to legislate an amendment to the national wage law, but cannot rely on Congress alone to do that job. Without a great national struggle there is small likelihood that Congress will do the right thing. It will take great pressure from all over the country and many segments of society to assure that the bill will be given serious consideration. It will take a major organizing effort, involving scores of local organizations of all kinds, community associations, trade unions, religious bodies, single issue organizations and others working to spread the idea through public meetings, petitions, demonstrations and other activities. If we organize broadly and effectively and mobilize the people, we can make Congress act.

We reach out to organizations, religious groups, trade unions and others to come together to become initiating sponsors of a national coalition to win a living wage for all. The way we propose to do it is open for discussion in such a coalition and the bill can be modified or changed by the coalition majority. We reach out with confidence that a majority of the people supports a living wage as fair and just.

The great 1999 demonstration in Seattle against the World Trade Organization and the pervasive abuses of capital's integrated global economy, marks the start of a powerful next wave of struggle for economic justice, for both saving and expanding democracy, for preservation of the environment and for survival and a decent life for the world's working majority. Seattle brought together an irresistible coalition of trade unions, community and human rights groups, environmentalists, people of color, women's and youth groups and many others. At the core of the protest was a deepening grasp of how the wild flight of capital around the world is aimed, among other things, at seeking the cheapest labor markets, and thus putting a stranglehold on the wages and living standards of working people in every part of the globe.

The outcry in Seattle against the antidemocratic and exploitative policies of the WTO inevitably embraces the fight for a living wage. A living wage is indeed at the heart of the emerging worldwide fight back against the depredations of the global system. Seattle has also given us a message: despite the awesome power of global capital and its domestic allies, a united majority of working people does indeed have the power to wring concessions, to roll back corporate greed, and ultimately to bring about a just, fair and democratic economy and polity. The living wage campaign is an inseparable part of that great process. *Let us win a national living wage.*

"Mandating living wages is not the most effective way to help low-wage workers."

Living Wage Ordinances Reduce Employment

Jill Jenkins

With the intention of raising the income level of low-wage workers, municipalities across the country have passed "living wage" ordinances that mandate pay levels significantly higher than the federal minimum wage. Jill Jenkins maintains in the following viewpoint that living wage ordinances will reduce employment opportunities for low-wage workers by forcing businesses to close or relocate to areas with lower costs. Low-wage workers would be better served by measures designed to improve their skills than by living wage ordinances, in the author's opinion. Jenkins is an economist with the Employment Policy Foundation, a public policy research organization focusing on workplace trends and policies.

As you read, consider the following questions:
1. How much above the federal minimum do living wage proponents want to raise wages, according to Jenkins?
2. In the author's opinion, to what age group do over half of all workers earning the minimum wage belong?
3. What are some of the transfer programs, according to the author, that boost the income and living standards of lower-wage workers?

Reprinted, with permission, from "The Unintended Consequences of 'Living Wages,'" by Jill Jenkins, *Employment Policy Foundation Fact & Fallacy*, vol. 5, no. 9 (November 23, 1999).

Arguing that the federal minimum wage is inadequate to help the working poor, community groups and unions across the country are promoting municipal "living wage" ordinances that mandate pay levels substantially above the federal minimum wage rate. The movement began in 1994 when Baltimore passed the first living wage ordinance, but precursors date as early as 1989. Currently, 40 municipalities (cities, counties, and school districts) have passed living wage policies and many more have campaigns under way or proposals on the table. Specific features vary from ordinance to ordinance and proposal to proposal, but typical ordinances cover employees of local government contractors and/or businesses receiving financial assistance from the local government. . . .

Living wage proponents advocate wages ranging from 20 to 100 percent or more above the current federal minimum wage of $5.15. With wage floors significantly higher than the national minimum wage, there are significant adverse effects of local living wage ordinances. These adverse consequences are compounded by their application only within the designated local area, shifting economic growth to outlying areas. Perhaps the most severe consequence is that living wages may not help the intended beneficiaries and may actually worsen their situations. Other policies are available that would more directly and less expensively help workers and their families improve their living standards. Living wage proponents have based their case on a series of misconceptions that are assessed in this viewpoint.

Poor Families Won't Benefit

The goal of living wage proponents is to raise the income level of lower-wage workers. They portray lower-wage earners as adult heads of low-income families. Neither view is correct.

According to Bureau of Labor Statistics (BLS) data, over half (51 percent) of all workers earning the minimum wage or below are young adults aged 16 to 24 years. Even more telling, 30.4 percent of workers earning the minimum wage or below are teenagers aged 16 to 19. . . . Individuals living with their parents make up the largest group of minimum wage earners (35.1 percent). Most of these individuals are teenagers or young adults, but the category also includes older "children" who do not live independently. In fact, family heads living with relatives account for less than 25 percent of minimum wage workers.

The lack of full-time, steady work opportunities, not low hourly wage rates, are at the core of poor families' low incomes. Few minimum wage earners are members of low-income families. At the time of the 1990 federal minimum wage increase, only 22 percent of affected workers lived in families with incomes below the poverty threshold. Most affected workers (53 percent) were actually living in families with incomes at least twice the poverty threshold. Thus, raising wage rates seems to be an inefficient way to raise the income level of poorer families.

Unrealistic Income Assumptions

Living wage advocates calculate the earnings of a minimum wage worker by simply multiplying the federal minimum wage ($5.15) by full-time work hours (2,000) to estimate an annual income of $10,300. This is indeed below the U.S. Census Bureau's poverty threshold for a family of four, but this comparison is misleading because it is based on unrealistic assumptions. First, it presumes that there is only one worker in a family. If a family consists of even two minimum wage earners, their before-tax income rises to $20,600, well above the poverty threshold for a family of two ($10,972 if under 65). It is also sufficient to put a family with up to three other persons above the poverty threshold. These income calculations are based on a 40-hour work week and do not include potential overtime earnings, at 150 percent of base salary, or the possibility of additional jobs (minimum wage or otherwise). If each adult in a four-person family works an additional 5 hours per week, family income increases by $3,862 to $24,462, which is 64 percent of U.S. median family income for 1997–1998.

Second, federal transfer programs, including food stamps, the Earned Income Tax Credit (EITC), housing subsidies, and school lunch programs, add significantly to the effective disposable income and living standards of lower-wage workers. Employer provided benefits are also received by approximately 52 percent of individuals earning a full-time minimum wage income. Figure 1 shows our estimates of the effective disposable income of various single minimum wage earner families once subsidies and expected employer benefits are included. When these are taken into account, families of up to four (including both single and dual-adult families) with only one minimum wage earner are raised above the poverty threshold. For example, a nuclear family with two children and only one minimum wage earner makes $22,356 after EITC, food stamps, child care deductions, housing subsidies, and expected employer benefits are taken into account.

Living Wages Will Cost Jobs

Living wage proponents deny that higher wage floors reduce employment. Repeated studies have shown significant employment losses associated with increases in the federal minimum wage. For example, a 1998 study by Burkhauser, Couch, and Wittenberg found that raising the minimum wage reduces employment among teenagers and young adults, with a 10 percent increase in the minimum wage leading to employment losses of 1.3 percent. Likewise, they found that a 10 percent increase in the minimum wage causes employment losses of 0.9 percent among adults aged 25 to 61. A 1992 study by Neumark and Wascher observed similar disemployment effects for teenage employment, and found that overall employment decreased 1.5 to 2 percent with a 10 percent increase in the minimum wage. The greatest negative impact falls on workers with the lowest levels of education and skills.

Furthermore, these studies examined mandated federal minimum wage increases, not local living wage increases. Even the most recent proposed minimum wage increase is only one-fifth the size of some living wage increases. Hence, even small disemployment effects at the national level are magnified by the size of local living wage increases. For example, using the conservative Burkhauser, Couch, and Wittenberg results, doubling the minimum wage would lead to employment decreases of 9.2 percent among adults and 14.7 percent among teenagers.

Living Wages Will Cause Businesses to Relocate

Living wage proponents the Association of Community Organizations for Reform Now (ACORN) believe that the "majority of low wage workers are employed in industries that are tied to their locations," such as food, transportation, or janitorial services that must be located near their customers in a central location, such as a city, to operate profitably. For this reason, they believe that the relocation consequences of living wages are minimal.

Family Income with One Full-Time $5.15 Minimum Wage Worker

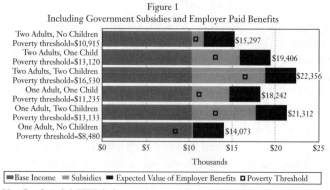

Figure 1
Including Government Subsidies and Employer Paid Benefits

Two Adults, No Children Poverty threshold=$10,915	$15,297
Two Adults, One Child Poverty threshold=$13,120	$19,406
Two Adults, Two Children Poverty threshold=$16,530	$22,356
One Adult, One Child Poverty threshold=$11,235	$18,242
One Adult, Two Children Poverty threshold=$13,133	$21,312
One Adult, No Children Poverty threshold=$8,480	$14,073

Thousands

■ Base Income   ■ Subsidies   ■ Expected Value of Employer Benefits   □ Poverty Threshold

Note: Benefits include EITC, food stamps, child care deductions, and housing subsidies, but not potential medicaid and other health benefits. A family with one full-time (2,000 hours) minimum wage worker earns $10,300 per year. All poverty thresholds are determined using a householder under 65 years of age.

Employment Policy Foundation, *Fact & Fallacy*, November 23, 1999.

However, even under these circumstances businesses may still close. Higher wage mandates will raise customer costs, as with taxes for government services. These customers may themselves relocate to areas where costs are lower, thereby decreasing employment opportunities for lower-wage individuals. Also, firms with low profit margins may abandon their businesses if labor costs inhibit their ability to operate profitably. The assistant vice president for the Prince George's County [Maryland] Chamber of Commerce, Robert M. Zinsmeister, expressed concern about precisely these effects in a recent interview. He stated that several businesses are already uneasy about Prince George's County's proposed living wage ordinance and are considering relocation.

Without job growth, a municipality cannot sustain a growing population. In fact, Mr. Zinsmeister also notes that some businesses are already reconsidering their decision to open operations in Prince George's County. Hence, these well-intentioned plans could start a cycle of economic stagnation or fuel already existing deterioration.

Applying More Effective Strategies

Mandating living wages is not the most effective way to help low-wage workers. Other strategies are more effective and will cause fewer adverse consequences.

For example, the Earned Income Tax Credit (EITC) is a better-targeted and more effective way of improving the earnings of low-wage working individuals and families, because it provides an income subsidy for these families. The EITC rewards work, rather than serving as a barrier to work, as is the case with a high living wage. In fact, a highly contentious debate over a living wage bill in Montgomery County, Maryland was recently defused when the county council voted unanimously to approve the nation's first local version of the EITC, providing credits of $176 to households with incomes below $17,000 per year. This figure will increase to $332 over the next two years. Elimination of the current family bias in the federal EITC could improve its effectiveness by lifting all individuals working nearly full-time, year-round out of poverty, regardless of their family status. Reducing or refunding a portion of payroll taxes for low-wage workers also provides an effective wage improvement strategy.

Living wage proposals are poorly focused and may actually hurt the intended beneficiaries. Job losses will fall most heavily on those with the lowest skill and education levels and only a fraction of the benefits will accrue to the intended recipients—low-income families. This is because living wage proposals focus on lower-wage earners, of whom the largest group is youth still living with relatives.

Many lower-wage workers lack education and job skills. Over 40 percent of minimum wage workers have less than a high school education, a much higher share than can be accounted for by their age distribution. As the returns to education and skills continue to grow, those with few marketable skills will face increasing difficulties. Rather than adopting living wage mandates that will likely further limit these individuals' job opportunities, measures designed to improve their workplace skills may ultimately be more effective.

Finally, living wage ordinances should be seen, not as a means of helping the poor, but as a "tool for union organizing." Many ordinances require contracting employers to be neutral in union organizing campaigns and to recognize unions based on card checks.

"Do we want software jobs—the putative hot career in today's economy—to permanently be occupied by foreign labor?"

Increasing the Number of Foreign Professionals Will Hurt U.S. Workers

Norman Matloff

H-1B work visas allow skilled foreigners to work in the United States for up to six years. In October 2000, Congress voted to increase the number of such visas issued annually to 195,000. Norman Matloff argues in the following viewpoint that the influx of H-1B workers is harmful and unnecessary. He contends that the computer industry has misled Congress with false claims of a skilled worker shortage in order to take advantage of cheap foreign labor. As a result, U.S. computer programmers are being shut out of the computer industry as software jobs increasingly become occupied by foreigners, in the author's opinion. Matloff is a professor of computer science at the University of California, Davis.

As you read, consider the following questions:
1. How does Matloff respond to the computer industry's claim that the education system is not producing enough programmers?
2. According to Matloff, why is the computer industry's labor shortage a permanent condition?
3. How does the author support his contention that it does not make good business sense to hire foreign labor?

Reprinted, with permission, from "The Computer Industry Finds That Scare Tactics Work," by Norman Matloff, *Intellectual Capital*, March 16, 2000, published at www.intellectualcapital.com.

The computer industry—possessing public-relations prowess worthy of the tobacco lobby—knows exactly which buttons to push to scare Congress. Its latest gamut [was pressuring] Congress into approving yet another increase in the quota for the H-1B work visa, mainly to hire foreign computer programmers. To do so they employed many arguments. There was the time-honored Education Button ("Our schools are failing to produce enough computer programmers"), the Overseas Industry Button ("If we can't bring foreign programmers here," we'll have to ship software work abroad"), and so on.

Members of Congress may think they understand the issues in the tobacco case, but as non-techies they are much less qualified to gauge the computer industry's claims—and they seem to realize that. Yet there is a simple, 10-minute experiment anyone can perform to assess the high-tech industry's claims. Simply call the Human Resources Department (HR) of any computer industry firm, large or small, and ask them four questions:

Straight Talk from HR

1. "How many programmers apply for positions with your firm each week?"

HR will cite a large number.

2. "How many of those do you invite for an in-person interview?"

HR will cite a small number.

3. "Why do you interview so few of your applicants?"

HR will reply that the vast majority of applicants are "unqualified," because they do not have experience with certain newer software skills, say the Java programming language.

4. "If an experienced programmer takes a course in Java to update his/her skills, would you extend an invitation to interview?"

HR will answer, "No, we need to hire someone with actual work experience, so that they can be productive from Day One."

Do that, and you can cut right through the lobbyists' rhetoric and reveal the true situation.

First, it shows that there is no shortage of programmers

after all. The problem is that employers are extremely picky as to whom they hire. Thus the industry's claim that the educational system is not producing enough programmers is patently false; the industry is only using a fraction of those we already have. This pickiness in hiring also completely belies the employers' claim that they are "desperate" to hire.

Training and Education, Not More H-1B Visas

The H-1B debate should not focus on an alleged skills or worker shortage, but instead focus on government and industry investment in the resources of U.S. workers. This readily available and qualified workforce remains neglected during this debate. . . . The record of the Information Technology (IT) industry in training its own workers, and facilitating the training of others outside its workforce is pathetic. There is no evidence of a comprehensive training strategy targeted at current or future skills shortages that the IT industry has developed or implemented. The industry has been conspicuously silent when job training policy and legislation has been proposed or debated by the Administration and Congress. Instead, the IT industry has invested its time and energy and wasted the time of policy and lawmakers by pursing the false solution of evermore H-1B workers. It is high time that we shift the focus of our national conversation to those workers with the requisite IT skills, or with skills that can be upgraded with limited training.

Congressional Testimony of David A. Smith, August 5, 1999.

Second, it shows that programming careers are short-lived, with the older programmers being forced to leave the field when their skills become obsolete. As a result, attrition in the programming field is far higher than in other technical fields, say civil engineering. Twenty years after graduation, only 19% of computer science graduates are still working as programmers, yet 52% of civil engineering graduates are still in the field at that time.

An Equal Employment Opportunity Commission (EEOC) report in an age discrimination lawsuit found that in the firm's layoff action, the termination rate for programmers over 40 was 10 times higher than for those under 40. The industry cites low-unemployment rates for programmers, but these are meaningless, since most programmers leave the field when they cannot find programming work. (In the lawsuit above, the former programmers were working in jobs such as truck drivers.)

Most importantly, the exercise with HR departments exposes the dishonesty in the lobbyists' central claim. They say that the H-1B program is just a temporary solution while the educational system gears up to produce more programmers. Yet HR's answers to the questions above show that the claimed labor "shortage" will be permanent, not temporary. The technology will always change rapidly, rendering today's "hot" software skill worthless a few years from now. So, no matter how many programmers the schools produce, it will always be the case that the vast majority of programmers will become "unqualified" in the eyes of the employers, say, 10 years after graduation.

The Heart of the Matter

This then becomes the fundamental issue that Congress should address: Do we want software jobs—the putative hot career in today's economy—to permanently be occupied by foreign labor?

What great attraction does foreign labor have for employers? As seen earlier, the answer involves specific software skills, both for insincere and sincere employers.

Insincere employers use the skills issue as a pretext for hiring H-1Bs at below-market rates, exploiting gaping loopholes in the "prevailing wage" portion of H-1B law. This has been established by several university studies, including one by an immigration attorney. A Department of Labor audit found that 19% of all H-1Bs were not even being paid the wage levels promised by their employers on the visa applications.

Even a *Wall Street Journal* article that had claimed that H-1Bs do not adversely affect job opportunities for American programmers stated that American firms recruit abroad because "recruiting foreign talent is cheaper than hiring Americans." An American recruiter profiled in the article said that he pays the foreign programmers $20,000 to $25,000 less than Americans with the same skills. Sincere employers who hire H-1Bs typically do so out of a genuine, though misguided, notion that they "must" hire someone with work experience in, say, Java. This does not make good business sense, as it would take a veteran programmer only a couple of weeks to become productive in Java, learning on the job.

The industry grants that veteran programmers can learn new skills on the job, but claims they need people who can be productive from the minute they are hired. Yet this claim is undermined by the industry's own admission that jobs are typically open for months before the employers find someone with the exact skill set they want.

Twisting the Issues

To be sure, we should indeed facilitate the immigration of "the best and the brightest" from around the world, but the vast majority of H-1Bs are not in this league. Department of Labor data show that 79% of the H-1Bs make under $50,000 per year, hardly what "geniuses" get in this field.

The lobbyists have twisted every issue—education, salaries, entrepreneurship, the threat of shipping software work overseas, and so on—beyond recognition. . . .

High-tech work is a locomotive of growth for our economy. But that locomotive works just as well when driven by U.S. citizens and permanent residents. The industry should hire them, rather than forcing them to leave the field.

> *"Of all the foreign workers coming to the U.S., no category provides such an instant boost to the economy as do H-1B [visa] professionals."*

Increasing the Number of Foreign Professionals Will Not Hurt U.S. Workers

Suzette Brooks Masters and Ted Ruthizer

In the following viewpoint, Suzette Brooks Masters and Ted Ruthizer assert that H-1B visas allowing skilled foreigners to work in the United States have added to the competitiveness of U.S. companies and contributed to the nation's economic success. Contrary to critics of increasing the number of H-1B visas issued annually, there is no evidence that the influx of foreign workers is displacing U.S. computer workers or depressing wages, according to the authors. Masters is an attorney and serves on the board of directors of the National Immigration Forum. Ruthizer is an immigration lawyer and general counsel of the American Immigration Lawyers Association.

As you read, consider the following questions:
1. What are the advantages to employers in hiring H-1B workers, in the authors' opinion?
2. According to Masters and Ruthizer, how many information technology workers will be needed through the year 2006?
3. What arguments do the authors make against claims that H-1B workers depress wages for Americans?

For almost 50 years, the U.S. economy has benefited from the contributions of H-1B foreign-national professionals. These persons are highly qualified professional workers who have been authorized to work for American employers on a temporary basis, not to exceed six years. When no suitable individual is available domestically, the H-1B visa has allowed businesses to use capable and often exceptional professionals from abroad in a wide range of fields, including information technology, finance, and science. In today's booming economy, as U.S. employers struggle to find enough skilled professionals, the H-1B program helps assure continued economic prosperity. Without major increases in this vital immigration status, the competitiveness of U.S. companies in the global marketplace will be undermined.

Meeting the Needs of Employers

The U.S. is the economic envy of the world. A dynamic tradition of accepting and successfully integrating successive waves of immigrants has made it the beneficiary of the world's most talented and renowned scientists, economists, engineers, mathematicians, computer scientists, and other professionals. Those immigrants have made major contributions, particularly in the high-tech sector. Recent studies that have measured the magnitude of those contributions have confirmed that immigration creates wealth and increases the size of the economy overall.

Of all the foreign workers coming to the U.S., no category provides such an instant boost to the economy as do H-1B professionals. Unlike their permanent counterparts, they offer the advantage of enabling employers to meet immediate labor needs. Employers can hire H-1Bs in months or even weeks. In contrast, it can take four years or more to qualify someone for permanent green card status. With unemployment at a peacetime, postwar low of four percent, the resulting tight labor market has made the H-1B status even more important to U.S. companies of all sizes.

Perhaps no industry presents a stronger case for increased usage of H-1Bs than does information technology (IT). The evidence is overwhelming that there is currently a serious shortage in the U.S. of IT professionals, one that is projected to become even more severe over the next several years. The Information Technology Association of America released a study in April, 2000, which showed that there are 850,000 high-tech job vacancies nationwide.

The explosive growth of high-tech jobs will likely continue through the next decade. In a June, 1999, study, the U.S. Department of Commerce underscored the importance of the IT sector to the economy, predicting that 1,400,000 new workers, or nearly 250,000 a year, would be required to meet the projected demand for information technology workers through 2006. Similarly, the Department of Labor projects the need for 200,000 new hires per year in the high-tech sector for each of the next 10 years.

Limits Inhibit Growth

The H-1B visa category was designed to be an asset to American industry, and for almost 40 years there was no limit on the number of H-1B petitions granted in any given year. In its 1992 report, the General Accounting Office stated that H-1B visas enable U.S. businesses to compete for international talent. Thus, their relative availability can help or hinder successful global competition.

The Immigration Act of 1990 erected a major competitive barrier for U.S. companies by imposing, for the first time, an annual cap of 65,000 on H-1B visas. The cap was first reached in 1997. In 1998, it was reached again, this time in May. Finally, in October, 1998, Congress responded to the employer outcry by enacting the American Competitiveness and Workforce Improvement Act, which increased the number of H-1B professionals to 115,000 for Fiscal Years (FY) 1999 and 2000, and to 107,500 for FY01. Because of pent-up demand and an economy chugging along in high gear, the increased numbers for FY99 were once again exhausted by the spring of 1999, and the Immigration and Naturalization Service (INS) even issued 25,000 more visas than permitted by the cap. In FY00, the situation was even worse—the 115,000 cap was reached in March. . . .

When the demand for workers cannot be met domestically, which is the case today, companies must look elsewhere. Ideally, they would hire foreigners and integrate them into their existing U.S. operations. However, if American companies are unable to gain access to the people they need because of limits on H-1B hiring, some are left with just one choice—hire the workers they require abroad with a corresponding offshore shift in domestic operations. This phenomenon, known as offshore outsourcing, can be harmful to the U.S. economy and American workers, especially in the more knowledge-intensive industries, because of the positive effect hiring skilled individuals can have on job creation and the economy.

Highly skilled workers are able to create new products and, in some cases, entire new sectors of an industry, affording opportunities for other workers. T.J. Rodgers, president and CEO of Cypress Semiconductors, testified before Congress that, for every foreign-born engineer he is allowed to hire, he can employ five other workers in marketing, manufacturing, and other related areas. At Sun Microsystems, both the Java computer language and the innovative SPARC microprocessor were created by engineers first hired through the H-1B program. Their endeavors then opened opportunities for thousands of others.

In the critical IT sector, companies that can't hire the professionals they need are going abroad in increasing numbers. In recent testimony before the Senate Subcommittee on Immigration investigating this problem, witness after witness spoke to that phenomenon. One prominent Internet executive testified that denying companies the ability to hire H-1B professionals leaves them three options: limiting the firms' growth, "stealing" employees from competitors, or moving operations offshore.

A Lack of Complaints

The most common argument against H-1Bs is that they allegedly displace American workers and depress wages. In response, Congress has spun an elaborate web of laws resulting in complex regulations, supposedly to protect native workers from any such impact. Yet, nothing in theory, wage and job trends, or law enforcement data indicates that the H-1B status has a negative effect on the U.S. labor market.

The Department of Labor (DOL), one of the major critics of the H-1B status, has carefully tracked the program's so-called abuses. We obtained and reviewed H-1B enforcement data from DOL and found that, from 1991, the inception of the H-1B caps, through 1999, it received a total of 448 complaints alleging underpayment of H-1B professionals and other employer violations (an average of fewer than 60 complaints nationwide each year). During that period, nearly 525,000 H-1B non-immigrant petitions were granted. The complaint rate for a program supposedly rife with abuse is minuscule.

Projected H-1B Demand

This chart demonstrates the need to increase the H-1B cap enough to account for projected demand over fiscal years (FY) 1999–2003. These projections are calculated from a base of 85,000 which represents FY98 demand. If the economy continues at its current pace, most immigration experts predict at least a 20% increase in demand over each of the next several fiscal years.

Fiscal Year	Growth in H-1B Demand				
	10%	15%	20%	25%	30%
FY99	93,500	97,750	102,000	106,250	110,500
FY00	102,850	112,413	122,400	132,813	143,650
FY01	113,135	129,274	146,880	166,015	186,745
FY02	124,449	148,666	176,256	207,520	242,769
FY03	136,893	170,965	211,507	259,399	315,599

Congressional Testimony of Austin T. Fragomen Jr., August 5, 1999.

A violation was found in 134 of the DOL investigations that have been completed to date. Back wages due over the entire eight-year period amounted to about 80 cents for every $100,000 paid in wages and salaries. Infractions of DOL wage roles are not only rare, but random, with no discernible pattern of intentional abuse. Of the 134 violations, just seven were determined to be "willful," an average of about one intentional violation per year.

What is most striking about the low level of enforcement activity is that an aggrieved party (i.e., the largely mythical American worker who loses a job to an underpaid temporary foreign worker) has but to make a call to DOL to start the ball rolling. Complaints don't require lawyers, simply a phone call. Workers talk to one another, and job-hopping is commonplace. If abuse were prevalent, it would be impossible to hide.

The Low-Wage Myth

Despite the absence of evidence that H-1B workers are paid less than the market wage, critics persist in arguing that they receive less than their American counterparts, which exerts downward pressure on wages. The facts are that wage growth is strong in the U.S. and that H-1B professionals' pay is on a par with that of their domestic counterparts. We know that H-1B workers are paid well because the law mandates that they must receive at least the prevailing wage or the actual wage paid to those who are similarly situated. Reviewing the enforcement evidence shows that an overwhelming majority of employers of H-1B workers are complying with the law. Given the desperate need employers have for skilled individuals, the high costs associated with H-1B hiring, and the extremely low incidence of violations detected by the Department of Labor, there is no basis for speculating that foreign-national workers are being paid less than the going rate.

Compound that with the fact that H-1B professionals are but a tiny fraction of the American labor force, and claims of wage erosion become increasingly fanciful. The stock of H-1B professionals in the U.S. (about 525,000) accounts for about one-third of one percent of the domestic workforce, which exceeds 140,000,000. With a labor market this large, at least 90,000 people change jobs every day. In this context, the effect of H-1B professionals on the overall labor market is insignificant.

In 1999, the Commerce Department reviewed the major competing sources of wage and salary data. It concluded with respect to IT workers—the sector that H-1B critics claim has been most harmed by the H-1B professionals—that wages have been high and rising, and that those with hot skills have been seeing faster salary growth. U.S. employers are paying top dollar to hire and retain the right workers and believe the investment is worthwhile.

Employers don't petition for H-1B professionals on a whim. The statutory and regulatory maze through which they must navigate is difficult, time-consuming, and expensive. To handle the complex H-1B process, employers generally must use specialized immigration counsel, knowledgeable human resources staff, compensation and benefits experts, and educational evaluators well-versed in reviewing foreign degrees and credentials. For each petition, the INS charges a $610 filing fee, $500 of which supports American worker retraining and scholarships. In addition, the employer must pay the expense of recruitment and, in many cases, help pay relocation costs for the employee and any immediate family members. After the expiration of the initial three-year H-1B petition, the employer must begin the H-1B process anew.

Not surprisingly, employers uniformly bemoan the high cost and difficulty of hiring H-1B professionals. According to Michael Murray, an executive at Microsoft, the costs of finding and employing foreign workers greatly exceed domestic hiring expenses and can run as high as $10–15,000 per employee. If Americans with the right skills were available, employers would be crazy not to hire them.

Strong Support for Training and Education

Another charge against the H-1B program is that it discourages U.S. companies from adapting to the domestic skill shortages by investing in training of the domestic workforce. In practice, though, American industry is pouring money into training programs and technical education. Phyllis Eisen, executive director of the National Association of Manufacturers' Center for Workforce Success, indicates that U.S. industry currently invests $60–80,000,000,000 in training annually.

The reasons for training are obvious: retaining existing employees, keeping pace with new product lines and technological advances, and boosting skill levels of new hires. U.S. companies are not only training their employees, but also educating America's youth to create a suitably trained workforce for the future.

Eliminate the Caps

Meanwhile, on Capitol Hill, Congress struggled to achieve consensus on whether and how much to raise the H-1B cap, largely ignoring the overwhelming evidence that attempts to "control" the H-1B inflow are not only unnecessary, but counterproductive. The American Competitiveness in the 21st Century Act, introduced by Orrin Hatch (R.-Utah) and Spencer Abraham (R.-Mich.) [became law in October 2000 and] raised the cap on H-1B visas to 195,000 [per year] . . . and increased the visa fee to $1,000. . . .

Since the evidence does not support claims of job displacement, wage erosion, or failure to invest domestically in training, what is the real fear of eliminating H-1B caps? Will millions of H-1B professionals invade America's shores? That outcome is extremely unlikely. Before 1990, there were no caps on H-1B entrants, and the numbers were always modest. In fact, it was not until 1997 that the legislated cap of 65,000 was met. Market conditions determine demand, not an arbitrarily legislated cap. The main impact of an H-1B cap during a time of high demand for skilled workers is to force American companies to relocate some of their operations overseas, thus reducing domestic job growth over what it would otherwise have been.

Indeed, the U.S. has been able to create more jobs than any other wealthy nation in part due to its ability to attract the world's best and brightest minds. Ironically, at the very time Congress is arguing about how to tinker with the cap, other countries have finally figured out how to welcome skilled workers to their shores. Germany and the United Kingdom are launching programs to tap the pool of skilled migrants through new streamlined procedures and special visas. In a global marketplace where skilled employees are in short supply, nations will be forced to compete for them. The U.S. would be foolish to forgo its strategic advantage by unduly restricting the flow of skilled workers to this country.

Periodical Bibliography

The following articles have been selected to supplement the diverse views presented in this chapter. Addresses are provided for periodicals not indexed in the *Readers' Guide to Periodical Literature*, the *Alternative Press Index*, the *Social Sciences Index*, or the *Index to Legal Periodicals and Books*.

Bruce Bartlett	"The Minimum Wage Trap," *Wall Street Journal*, April 16, 1996.
Michael Bernick	"Welfare Reform: It's Making Strides," *San Francisco Chronicle*, February 18, 1998.
Business Week	"From Welfare to Worsefare?" October 9, 2000.
Christian Science Monitor	"Harvard Sit-In Asks for a 'Living Wage,'" April 24, 2001.
Tom Delay	"Putting People to Work Privately," *Washington Times*, March 16, 1997.
Christina Duff	"Why a Welfare 'Success Story' May Go Back on the Dole," *Wall Street Journal*, June 15, 1999.
Laura Dykes	"Living-Wage Laws Hurt Poor the Most," *Los Angeles Business Journal*, March 26, 2001.
The Economist	"Freedom from Want: A Century of Surprises as Work Force Changed," *San Diego Union-Tribune*, December 19, 1999.
James O. Goldsborough	"How France Deals with Unemployment," *San Diego Union-Tribune*, October 28, 1999.
Bob Herbert	"Disparities at Harvard," *New York Times*, April 30, 2001.
Edward L. Hudgins	"Vacation from Sanity," *Daily Commentary*, Cato Institute, July 10, 2000. Website: www.cato.org//dailys/07-10-00.html.
Mickey Kaus	"Workfare's Misguided Critics," *New York Times*, May 5, 1998.
Carrie Kirby	"H-1B Visa Program Crucial to Economy, Study Says," *San Francisco Chronicle*, October 25, 2000.
Robert Kuttner	"Making Sure Workers Live Decently," *San Diego Union-Tribune*, August 17, 1997.
Patricia Ann Lamoureux	"Is a Living Wage a Just Wage?" *America*, February 19, 2001.

Sam Mistrano   "Welfare Clock Will Run Out Before Job Supply Catches Up," *Los Angeles Times*, July 16, 1999.

Bobbi Murray   "Money for Nothing," *Los Angeles Times Magazine*, vol. 45, no. 11, November 2000.

Robert B. Reich   "It's the Year 2000 Economy, Stupid," *American Prospect*, January 3, 2000.

Richard Rothstein   "Questioning the Labor Shortage for High Tech Workers," *New York Times*, September 6, 2000.

Peter J. Sammon   "The Living Wage Movement: There Are 20 Campaigns Underway in Cities and Counties Nationwide," *America*, August 26, 2000.

Eugene Scalia   "A New Federal Mandate: Don't Work Too Hard," *Wall Street Journal*, March 1, 1999.

Donald J. Senese   "Government Intervention Creates Chaos, Not Jobs," n.d. Website: www.libertyhaven.com/ theoreticalorphilosophicalissues/conservatism/ govintervention.html.

Somini Sengupta   "Workfare Victory for a Recovering Addict Holds Promise for Others," *New York Times*, September 10, 2000.

Dan Stein   "What High-Tech Labor Shortage Is That?" *San Diego Union-Tribune*, June 25, 1998.

Peter Waldman   "The Outlook: Prosperity Is Good for Living Wage Drive," *Wall Street Journal*, December 20, 1999.

Leslie Wayne   "Workers, and Bosses, in a Visa Maze," *New York Times*, April 29, 2001.

Joanie Wexler   "Should the H-1B Cap Be Raised?" *Computerworld*, August 28, 2000.

Glenn Woiceshyn   "The Basis of Good Government: The Protection of Individual Rights," *Capitalism*, October 1999.

CHAPTER 3

What Role Should Labor Unions Play in the Workplace?

Chapter Preface

Since the membership highs of the 1950s, labor unions in the United States have struggled to find a footing in the workplace as the manufacturing sector of the economy, a traditional bastion of union support, has declined significantly. The high-tech global economy of the early twenty-first century—commonly referred to as the "new economy"—has made it increasingly difficult for labor unions to organize new members and influence the working and living standards of U.S. workers.

Labor leaders contend that unions are reasserting their relevancy to new economy workers by spending more time and money on community recruitment and education programs. These programs are intended to organize and create support networks for full-time, part-time, temporary, and contract workers facing an unstable job market. Explains Julie Kosterlitz, a writer for the *National Journal*, "[Workers] can still use help [from unions] . . . in securing retraining . . . and in . . . [obtaining] health and pension benefits." According to Kosterlitz, new economy workers have a need for independent advocates protecting them from exploitation, and labor unions are reconfiguring themselves to best provide that protection.

Other commentators assert that new economy job growth has been greatest in non-union white-collar jobs that have no tradition of union representation. Accustomed to looking out for their own interests in a mobile economy, the majority of workers occupying these positions consider union representation unnecessary. According to the Employment Policy Foundation, "Legislation has made it easier for individual workers to challenge . . . issues in which unions might have played an important role in the past." Where unions once fought against job discrimination and for better working conditions, expanded individual rights have enabled workers to settle grievances against employers on their own.

Whether unions will decline or undergo a resurgence is certain to have a sizable impact on the rapidly changing economy. The authors in the following chapter debate what role, if any, unions should play in the U.S. workplace.

"Union leaders, activists, and rank-and-file members are finally coming together to discuss and to initiate strategies at the local level to reverse the labor movement's decline."

The Influence of Labor Unions May Be Increasing

Amy B. Dean

Amy B. Dean maintains in the following viewpoint that labor unions are increasing their strength and membership numbers by developing innovative recruitment, training, and job placement programs at the local level. Under the Union Cities initiative, labor unions have turned to central labor councils to shape local economic development and mobilize community support for workers' rights, according to the author. In Dean's opinion, these efforts are enhancing the appeal of labor unions to workers in the new economy. Dean is executive officer of the South Bay AFL-CIO Labor Council and chairperson of the AFL-CIO's National Advisory Committee on the Future of Central Labor Councils.

As you read, consider the following questions:
1. According to Dean, what aspects of the "new economy" present a challenge for the labor movement?
2. In the author's opinion, how did John Sweeney and his supporters rebuild union power at the local level during their 1995 campaign?
3. In what three ways does the Union Cities initiative achieve its goal of establishing successful unions at the local level, in Dean's opinion?

Excerpted from "The Road to Union City: Building the Labor Movement Citywide," by Amy B. Dean, in *Not Your Father's Union Movement*, edited by Jo-Ann Mort. Reprinted by permission of Verso.

Richelle Noroyan is a twenty-five-year-old college graduate living in Santa Cruz, California. But, despite her education, all Noroyan's diploma ever bought her was a succession of seven dollar an hour jobs in the region's booming high-tech industry.

Several miles away, Alejandro Rodriguez and his family live in San Jose. For four years, Rodriguez, a refugee from Nicaragua, worked as a shipping clerk at Hewlett-Packard (HP). But two years ago, the giant computer maker subcontracted Rodriguez's job—and those of his co-workers—to a large temporary employment firm that provides few of the benefits HP offers its full-time employees. Though neither Noroyan and Rodriguez may know it, both represent the greatest challenge—and best hope—facing the American labor movement: the workers of the new economy. But winning their support and that of millions of other workers like them requires a re-engineering of the labor movement and a fundamental redefinition of its relationship to the communities in which it operates.

U.S. Unions and the New Economy

Globalization, new technologies, and a rapidly changing workforce demography have given way to a strange new economic landscape. Union leaders have long recognized the effect these forces could have on workers and their families and, over the course of the last twenty-five years, have offered a few responses to the challenges facing U.S. industries in the new economy. In 1964, for example, Walter Ruether of the United Auto Workers lobbied for a federal commitment to produce an American-made alternative in response to the growing demand for imported Volkswagens. In the time since Ruether proposed his federal response to auto imports, foreign trade has accelerated greatly, making the U.S. economy almost three times more dependent on it than it was in the early 1960s. The impact on workers and their unions has been catastrophic in many industries, and even the toughest restrictions on imports or the introduction of new technologies provide little resistance to the new world order. While many predicted that the end result of globalization and new technologies would be massive, permanent unemployment, time has proven that instead, many of the jobs lost in manufacturing and other industries have been replaced by jobs not unlike those held by Noroyan and Rodriguez. An earlier generation of Americans once looked for jobs in metal-bending industries, but today's workforce is more likely to seek jobs in information technology, the public sector, and health care. By the year 2005, there will be more than seven times as many Americans working as systems analysts than as tool and die makers. The number of workers employed in technical and related support positions will increase by more than 20 percent. Jobs in service occupations will expand by more than 18 percent. Yet while almost three-quarters of U.S. workers are already employed in these sectors, fewer than 13 percent are union members today. And no less significant to U.S. unions than these new kind of jobs is the economy that is creating them.

The New Localism

The growth of health care giants such as Columbia/HCA and Kaiser Permanente suggests the era of large corporate employers is anything but behind us, but big business is hardly the big employer it once was. As Alejandro Rodriguez's experience underscores, many firms, particularly in the information technology industry, prefer to subcontract tasks that may have previously been performed in-house. Unlike U.S. Steel, which operated its own coal mines, or Ford Motor, whose massive Rouge Assembly Plant was even built with resources from its own steel mill, a distinguishing characteristic of new businesses is their reluctance to invest in plants and personnel of their own. Instead, these firms depend on an intricate network of subcontractors who, in turn, regularly contract out work of their own. Similarly, as Richelle Noroyan's experience suggests, even professional and technical workers, who may have once built careers by working for only one employer, now find themselves working for several on a part-time or temporary basis. In the health care industry, for example, nurses and other technical employees routinely work as independent contractors. The fact that many of the new economy's workers will find employment at several firms in their community rather than at a large, multinational corporation presents a unique challenge for the U.S. labor movement.

Organizing the workers of the new economy means targeting a host of smaller local employers rather than a handful of large ones, as well as making union membership attractive to those workers who will frequently change employers. For example, many of the needs experienced by these workers, such as portable pension and health care benefits, job training and placement services, can be—and often are—provided through unions. Yet, doing so requires organized labor to become far less centralized and more interwoven with local community services than it is currently.

Unions Raise Wages

Median weekly earnings of full-time wage and salary workers, 1996

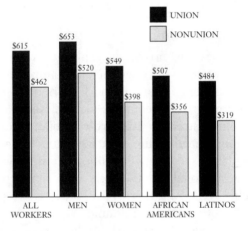

U.S. Bureau of Labor Statistics.

As federal power "devolves" to the state and local levels, representing workers in the new economy demands that unions become more integrated in local decision-making processes than they have ever been in the past. . . . Unions must have more significant responsibility or role in shaping local economic development.

To represent effectively workers like Noroyan and Rodriguez, unions will need to adopt structures as flexible and, as in many respects, as decentralized as the new economy itself. Some are. One of America's oldest unions, the International Association of Machinists & Aerospace Workers (IAM), has launched an innovative training program to help both local Machinist leaders and their employers decentralize decision-making to help transform companies into "high performance" workplaces. Other unions, once accustomed only to more traditional forms of collective bargaining, are seeking to become relevant to contingent workers by reinventing themselves. They can take their cue from unions in the performing arts, entertainment, and construction industry. One of the most promising initiatives is the Communications Workers of America's (CWA) effort to establish employment centers. Such centers combine placement services with skill certification, creating a labor market intermediary valued by both employees and employers in which the union has a major role in training, workforce development, and placement.

A Culture of Decline

There is, of course, no single explanation for the labor movement's failure to organize the unorganized either in the new or old economy. Many union leaders often point with good reason to the shortcomings of U.S. labor law. But the decline of union strength can hardly be blamed on weak labor laws alone. Challenging organized labor's culture of decline is fundamental to growing unions in the new economy. While most national labor leaders understand the importance of change, local leaders must take some responsibility for the real work of rebuilding union strength. It is here, in communities across America, where the new economy is taking shape and where the day-to-day political battles that will shape the future of U.S. workers will be fought. And, not incidentally, it's here, too, where over 80 percent of organized labor's resources—and all of its members—can be mobilized to meet that challenge.

For the better part of a decade, the process of grassroots change has been gathering momentum in cities like San Jose, Atlanta, Seattle, and Milwaukee. In these and other communities, union activists frequently sidestepped the American Federation of Labor-Congress of Industrial Organization (AFL-CIO) in the 1980s and early 1990s to organize local Jobs with Justice coalitions or other initiatives to win new allies for unions in the community. These coalitions, composed of unions, religious leaders, civil rights activists, and others, helped compensate for the labor movement's declining clout in contract negotiations and local politics. . . . But while evidence of a new, creative movement for economic justice could be found in many communities throughout the U.S., it ultimately took the Sweeney insurgency to galvanize organized labor's renaissance.

The New AFL-CIO

Though the drive that sent John Sweeney [president of the AFL-CIO], Richard Trumka, and Linda Chavez-Thompson to the AFL-CIO in 1995 was sparked by a general desire for change, the programs they've initiated have actually borrowed heavily from the labor movement's past. In several important respects, the Sweeney program is reminiscent of the early days of the Congress of Industrial Organizations (CIO), when the cause of unionism and social justice were seen as one and the same in many communities. However, where the CIO of the 1930s helped engineer massive organizing drives that targeted industries, Sweeney's AFL-CIO instead may become a catalyst for organizing entire regions. . . .

Where Sweeney and the "new" AFL-CIO have been able to seize the initiative is where it counts the most: at the local level.

Though even some of its friends describe the AFL-CIO as a mammoth Washington bureaucracy, it is also a collection of individual state-level federations and 600 central labor councils (CLCs). These semi-autonomous state federations and CLCs, many of which predate the AFL-CIO itself, all have their own histories and unique traditions. . . .

At one time, CLCs were the cornerstone of much of the American labor movement, when the distance and meager resources of national unions made routine servicing of their local affiliates difficult, if not impossible. It was a time when the absence of effective labor laws demanded that union activists band together for their very survival. In 1934, for example, the AFL's Minneapolis, Minnesota Central Labor

Union, joined with the Teamsters in a series of strikes so effective that the state's governor finally declared a "state of insurrection" and imposed martial law. In the years since, the activities of most CLCs have hardly been as noteworthy. . . . Lacking any clear mission or goals, CLCs in many communities have devolved into little more than social clubs for local union leaders, largely dormant organizations barely capable of organizing blood collection drives for the Red Cross, let alone the workers of the new economy.

The Road to Union City

The first indication that John Sweeney and his supporters understood the urgency of rebuilding union power at the local level came during their 1995 campaign. In the months leading up to the AFL-CIO's convention, Sweeney's team moved swiftly to take advantage of an obscure provision in the AFL-CIO Constitution providing each CLC with one convention delegate. Though the individual votes of these delegates would have no effect on a roll-call vote, Sweeney realized that the presence of hundreds of additional supporters on the convention floor could be an important factor in his behalf. The effort to solicit support for Sweeney from CLCs often turned into fierce battles that bitterly divided local labor councils. Yet this effort also gave rise, for the first time ever, to an identifiable group of CLC leaders backing change at the AFL-CIO.

In 1996, with Sweeney's support, these CLC leaders became the nucleus of a twenty-two member Advisory Committee on the Future of Central Labor Councils. Working with the AFL-CIO's staff, the members of the committee surveyed the current activities and goals of CLCs, but more importantly, debated strategies for the ways in which CLCs could re-engineer themselves to be effective organizations that could improve opportunities for unions to be successful in organizing and bargaining at the local level. Committee members understood that CLCs could become a vital force to promote organizing, to educate and to mobilize community support for workers' rights, and to give labor a stronger voice in the political arena. . . . But they also understood that, to be successful, they had to provide a framework that CLCs could use to plan and to measure their performance and progress. That framework became the Union Cities initiative.

The Union Cities initiative is a straightforward set of eight goals that the AFL-CIO presented as a challenge to CLCs and other labor bodies:

Shifting 30 percent of their resources to organizing. Currently, CLCs have essentially no role in promoting union growth. By urging them to commit one-third of their resources to organizing, the AFL-CIO has challenged them to assist unions to win new members. Some CLCs have responded by coordinating multi-union organizing "blitzes" (which are quick, intense organizing sessions where organizers either visit workers at their homes or at the plant gates or outside of the worksites), training volunteer member organizers, and generating political and community support for first time organizing drives and contract fights.

Mobilizing union members to participate in demonstrations and other "rapid response" efforts against anti-union employers. . . .

Organizing to elect pro-worker candidates for office and holding them accountable once they are elected. . . .

Promoting local economic development efforts that create jobs and honor community values. Given the growth of the new economy at the local level, CLCs are being encouraged to become directly involved in local economic development initiatives as advocates for workers and their families.

Sponsoring the AFL-CIO's new economics education program geared to union families. Winning the fight to gain strong contracts and organize new members is impossible unless union families understand the scope of the economic changes shaping their workplaces and communities. CLCs can now play a critically important role in raising the awareness of union families about these and other issues by sponsoring the Federation's innovative new economics education classes.

Urging local governments to pass measures supporting the right of workers to organize. By challenging local governments to support workers' rights, CLCs can help generate a local climate more conducive to union organizing.

Working to insure greater ethnic, racial, and gender diversity in all CLC operations. As has often been noted, the failure of the labor movement to reflect the diversity of the American workforce has seriously undermined its ability to attract new members. As the most visible voice of the labor movement at the local level, it is particularly crucial for CLCs to challenge the widespread notion that unions are principally the domain of white males.

Encouraging CLC's to work with unions to achieve a 3 percent growth rate by the year 2000. In the past, the AFL-CIO has presented CLCs with few goals to measure their progress. By setting a target of a 3 percent growth rate by the year 2000, the Federation has created a standard CLCs can use to measure their progress.

Reinvigorating the Labor Movement

In essence, the "eight steps" to becoming a Union City are intended to create the local environment necessary for unions to, once again, be successful in organizing and bargaining. Union Cities achieves this goal first, by bringing local unions together within a region to set objectives and to develop a strategic action plan to build their power and promote new growth. Second, by putting their Union Cities plan into action, a once sedentary local labor movement will become reinvigorated and once again be able to demonstrate the depth of its public support. Third, the local labor movement will then be able to form the broader alliances necessary to put the issues of economic equity and social justice front and center in the community as a whole. To date, more than one hundred CLCs representing almost half of all U.S. union members have endorsed the effort. Perhaps even more important than their endorsement, though, is the fact that even by considering it, union leaders, activists, and rank-and-file members are finally coming together to discuss and to initiate strategies at the local level to reverse the labor movement's decline. . . . And, if our experience in San Jose offers any guide, the debate being fostered by Union Cities will inevitably help organized labor live up to the challenge of organizing in the new economy.

By committing itself several years ago to a program not unlike Union Cities, San Jose's South Bay AFL-CIO Labor Council was able to move well beyond then-traditional boundaries of the labor movement. By engaging our own membership and the community, our CLC came to better understand what it would take for workers, like Richelle Noroyan and Alejandro Rodriguez, to begin to see organized labor as part of their future, not just their past. To reach out to these workers, we launched a new kind of coalition—Working Partnerships USA—to build bridges between organized labor and workers in the new economy. Through Working Partnerships, we are "reinventing" our own local labor movement with an eye toward offering high tech workers the representation and services they truly need, not the kind the labor movement believes they should want. While Working Partnerships USA may not be a model for CLCs in every community, it has enabled ours to become a far more relevant voice: one that resonates with working families as a whole, and not just organized labor's institutional base.

The left has traditionally mistaken localism for conservatism, but if the next generation of American unionism is to take root, it will be by rejecting "big labor" in favor of more decentralized, flexible approaches: a unionism contoured to respond to each region's unique economy and workforce. History may someday show that by launching Union Cities, John Sweeney did more than breathe new life into old central labor councils. He may have triggered an irreversible process that finally enabled the American labor movement to organize the workers of the new economy.

*"Unless union strategies change
dramatically, . . . America's private-sector
unions will be an interesting footnote in
our grandchildren's history classes."*

The Influence of Labor Unions Is Declining

Kevin Hassett

In the following viewpoint, Kevin Hassett argues that the self-destructive strategies of labor unions have convinced many U.S. workers that unions no longer provide valuable services. Union demands for higher wages and stricter work rules limit the productivity of U.S. companies, forcing firms to outsource production or move overseas, according to Hassett. In the author's opinion, the unwillingness of union leaders to adapt to a changing economic landscape threatens the survival of unions in America. Hassett is a resident scholar at the American Enterprise Institute, a public policy research organization dedicated to the preservation of free enterprise.

As you read, consider the following questions:
1. Since the 1950s, what has happened to firms and industries where organized labor holds significant power, according to Hassett?
2. In Hassett's opinion, how does the union "profit tax" make unionized firms less willing to purchase more efficient machines than nonunionized firms?
3. Why do unionized firms almost always merge with other unionized firms, in the author's opinion?

Reprinted, with permission, from "Vanishing Unions," by Kevin Hassett, *The American Enterprise*, September/October 1998. Copyright © 1998 by the American Enterprise Institute for Public Policy Research.

Are America's unions committing suicide? The organized labor movement as we know it started shortly after an 1842 Massachusetts court decision declared that strikes were not criminal conspiracies. Over the next 80 years, the unions could command considerable sympathy. When almost 400,000 workers went on strike in 1919—shortly after the American Federation of Labor organized much of the iron and steel industries—the conditions the workers sought to improve were appalling. Many worked 12-hour days, seven days a week, often in hot and dangerous conditions. While one can object to the actions of the famed Molly Maguires, a group of Irish coal miners who terrorized Pennsylvania's coal companies in the 1800s, the fact that working conditions could lead men to such desperate acts should disturb any observer.

The Unionized Workforce Shrinks

Against this sobering backdrop, the 1998 United Auto Workers strike at GM was pure farce. Most of GM's North American production ceased, following a strike at their Flint, Michigan metal fabricating center. One of the chief disputes was GM's objection to outdated piece-work rules that, combined with improvement in assembly-line efficiency, mean that workers often quit after a half-day of work with full pay—which averaged $69,000 in 1997, plus $29,000 of fringe benefits, the *New York Times* reported.

GM argues that such expensive labor practices drive up the cost of GM cars, which in turn could eventually drive the company out of business. Historical evidence suggests GM has a point: Firms and industries where organized labor has significant power have experienced a steady decline since the 1950s, while those sectors not controlled by unions have blossomed, benefiting labor and management alike. The net result has been one of the more dramatic reversals in U.S. economic history. According to data from the U.S. Bureau of Labor Statistics, the percentage of the private workforce that is unionized climbed from about 6.8 percent in 1930 to about 27 percent in the early 1950s, but then declined to below 10 percent by 1997. Twenty more years of this trend would take the percentage of private workers unionized to zero! (Unionized government workers are another story. In this sector, not known for watching costs or improving efficiency, union membership is growing.)

So why has unionization in the private sector declined? Economists who study unions point to several factors. The first piece of the puzzle is the effect of unions on the way workers are used and paid. Unionized workers earn, on average, about 15 percent more than nonunionized workers, according to a National Bureau of Economic Research study. Unions also negotiate with firms to create rules that are intended to improve working conditions. The piece-rate rules at the Flint plant are just one example.

Many union supporters argue that this negotiating power is valuable, because otherwise large firms would hold disproportionate power over workers. In the blind pursuit of profits, the argument goes, capitalists wring every last ounce of effort out of workers, without regard to the workers' welfare.

Raising Costs, Limiting Adaptability

On the other hand, higher wages and stricter work rules put an enormous burden on firms. Labor costs are a very high share of total costs for most firms. Take the average U.S. firm, increase its labor costs by 15 percent (as unionization typically does), and almost all of its profits would be eliminated.

What happens to a firm if unions force it to pay more for labor than its competitors pay? If the firm has a monopoly on its product, then it can simply pass the higher costs on to consumers. But if many other nonunionized firms sell exactly the same product, then the unionized firm may well go bankrupt quickly. In the real world, most unionized firms are, like GM, somewhere in between. They have significant market power, so there is some chance they can survive even when their costs rise; but they do not have so much market power that they can ignore the possibility of losing sales to competitors. For such a firm, the ability to adjust in order to maintain competitiveness is critical for its long-term survival. Yet not only do unions raise labor costs, but employers also complain that union rules make it difficult to adapt to changing technologies and market conditions.

Studies of the practices of unionized firms reveal the second clue to unions' demise: Firms are generally unable to overcome the costs of unionization. If unionization were a disease, it would be one for which there is no cure. Economists have investigated two potential avenues of adjustment: Unionized firms could purchase more machines, or they could expand by buying nonunionized firms outright. Neither approach seems to work.

© Huck/Konopacki Labor Cartoons. Used with permission.

Buying more machines has an intuitive appeal. Since unions increase wages, unionized firms could, in theory, automate their way to lower costs and thereby at least partly overcome the higher costs of union wages. In an article in the *Journal of Labor Economics*, Federal Reserve Economist Bruce C. Fallick and I show that this strategy has not helped U.S. firms. For when more efficient machines increase a firm's profits, unions increase their wage demands commensurately, in effect taxing away the profits from the machines. Because of this union "profit tax," unionized firms are in practice *less* willing to purchase new machines than nonunionized firms. How much less? We found that firms generally lower investment by about 30 percent when their workers are unionized—not a recipe for growth.

Unions' "Contagion Effect"

Alternatively, unionized firms have been accused of acquiring nonunion firms to get around higher wages and union work rules: If your plant in Massachusetts organizes, buy a firm that operates in Mississippi, and threaten to transfer work to the southern plant the next time you bargain with the Massachusetts union. Organized labor has pushed this scenario for some time. In testimony before the Senate Finance Committee in 1989, for example, [former] [American Federation of Labor and Congress of Industrial Organization [AFL-CIO] president Lane Kirkland claimed that 90,000 union members had lost their jobs in the previous decade because of such takeovers.

The facts do not agree. In another recent paper, Fallick and I look at a large sample of U.S. mergers and show that union firms almost always merge with other unionized firms, while nonunion firms almost always merge with nonunion firms. Why is the pattern the opposite of the unions' claims?

A simple example illustrates the problem faced by a union firm. Consider a convenience store with a nice location, nonunionized workforce, and a market value of a million dollars. What would happen to that value if the workers unionized? It would go down. Higher labor costs would lower current and future profits, and a buyer's willingness to pay would also decline. Now if a unionized firm looks at a nonunionized convenience store, it will worry that its union will spread to the new firm. Shortly after paying a million dollars for the new store, the spread of the union would significantly lower the new property's value. If the firm buys a unionized store, however, the union is already there, and there is less of a chance the asset will decline in value. This contagion effect is decisive, we found, which means that extracting concessions by transferring work to a nonunionized workforce is not an option for most employers.

The final potential adjustment for a firm is to outsource production either to nonunion suppliers or overseas. This strategy may well help the company survive, but it doesn't do much to ensure the survival of unions in America.

So it is easy to see why, in retrospect, the number of union employees in America has gradually declined. There is little firms can do to overcome the cost disadvantage imposed by higher union wages. If they try to modernize to increase productivity, unions increase wage demands. If they try to purchase a competitor's plant that operates more efficiently, the union spreads to the new plant and makes it less efficient.

American workers seem to understand this, which is the final piece of the declining unionization puzzle. After witnessing such disruptive absurdities as the GM strike, most Americans want little to do with unions, and efforts to unionize new plants are rarely successful. Indeed, a recent paper by Henry Farber and former Clinton administration economist Alan Krueger documents a striking decline in the demand for unionization by America's workers. Farber and Krueger hypothesize that Americans no longer want to be unionized because workers are more satisfied with their jobs and less convinced that unions provide valuable services.

When workers were working 12 hours a day, seven days a week over hot furnaces, the union movement had the moral high ground. When America's capitalists wised up, wages and working conditions became reasonable, and workers began to look critically at what unions accomplish. Rather than work to be constructive in the new environment, unions continued old strategies that were unreasonable, confrontational, and ultimately self-destructive. As unionized firms withered on the vine, America's workers recognized that unions' addiction to short-term gains ultimately carries a high long-term cost.

Unless union strategies change dramatically, recent trends will continue, and America's private-sector unions will be an interesting footnote in our grandchildren's history classes. Since union leaders never adjusted their approach to a changing world, the death will go down as a suicide.

| *"The labor movement . . . is hurt more than it is helped by reliance upon compulsion in attracting and retaining members."*

Workers Should Not Be Required to Pay Union Fees

Reed Larson

Federal law allows requiring all employees to pay union fees for collective bargaining services as a condition of employment in workplaces where the majority of workers are unionized. According to Reed Larson in the following viewpoint, forcing employees to pay union dues violates the principles of a free society by compelling them to pay financial tribute to a private association. A national right-to-work law would end the practice of forced unionism and dues collection and protect all U.S. workers from union officials, who, in Larson's opinion, exploit employees for power and profits. Larson is president of the National Right to Work Committee based in Springfield, Virginia.

As you read, consider the following questions:
1. According to Larson, how would the National Right to Work Act change the National Labor Relations Act?
2. What tactics do union officials deploy to prevent companies from becoming "open shops," according to the author?
3. Why should union leaders welcome national right-to-work legislation, in the author's opinion?

Reprinted from the written statement of Reed Larson to the U.S. House of Representatives, Committee on Education and the Workforce, Subcommittee on Oversight and Investigations, May 3, 2000.

B ecause of its complexity, our Federal Labor Law is not understood by most Americans. I'd like to open my testimony with a simple illustration that highlights the principle upon which the National Labor Relations Act rests.

Imagine yourself standing just outside this building when a cab pulls up. You get in with two other passengers. When the driver announces that the cab is on its way to Baltimore, you protest, but the other two passengers grab you and tie you up.

The driver and his two henchmen ignore your protests.

After an hour's drive, he finally pulls over. The car stops and they untie you. But before they let you go, your assailants grab your wallet and remove $40. "This is for cab fare," they explain.

You're incredulous. "You've got to be kidding," you say. "You forced me to go with you. I had nothing to say about it."

"But you don't understand," they tell you. "We had a vote and the majority rules. And unless you pay your share of the ride, you're a 'free rider.' We have every right to make you pay."

"But I didn't want to go to Baltimore," you say. "I'm a kidnap victim!"

In a nutshell, I have just illustrated how the National Labor Relations Act (NLRA) abuses the freedom of working people to earn an honest living for themselves and their families. Under this so-called "Magna Carta" of workers' rights, employees who never requested union representation are forced to accept a union as their monopoly bargaining agent. Then, adding insult to injury, under the Federal Labor Policy they are forced to pay for representation they never requested and do not want.

That the NLRA is often perceived as a great charter of freedom was not entirely unintentional on the part of its drafters. In fact, it contains some of the most deliberately misleading language human beings could devise. Let me read the essential portion of Section 7, cleverly entitled, "Rights of Employees":

> Employees shall have the right to self-organization to form, join, or assist labor organizations, to bargain collectively through representations of their own choosing, and to engage

in other concerted activities for the purpose of collective bargaining or other mutual aid or protection, and shall also have the right to refrain from any or all such activities. . . .

Now, what could sound fairer than that?

But wait—let me *finish* the sentence: Employees shall have the right to refrain *"except to the extent that such right may be affected by an agreement requiring union membership as a condition of employment. . . ."*

That "except," and the words that follow, have to be one of the most cynical exercises in legislative deception on record.

Ending Compulsory Unionism

The National Right to Work Act, legislation that has been introduced by Congressman Bob Goodlatte, would end this cynicism by deleting the above-quoted exception and its referenced language in Federal Law empowering union officials to force private-sector employees to pay union dues in order to work. *Not one letter is added to Federal law.*

There is no natural right in a free society for any private association to compel financial tribute. Only the federal government's preemption of labor-management relations in the private sector makes such coercion possible.

Even the most avid promoters of compulsory unionism are forced to defend it on the basis of pragmatism, not principle. They contend that an organization of compelled members is stronger and more effective.

No less an authority than our former Secretary of Labor, Robert Reich, put this most succinctly. As a Harvard lecturer in 1985, he gave the following explanation of Federal Labor Law to an Associated Press reporter—and I quote his *exact* words:

> In order to maintain themselves, unions have got to have some ability to strap their members to the mast.
>
> The only way unions can exercise countervailing power vis-à-vis management is to hold their members' feet to the fire. . . . Otherwise, the organization is only as good as it is convenient for any given member at any given time."

Robert Reich has accurately—if callously—described the basic principle of Federal Labor Law—that convenience of union officials must take precedence over the freedom of employees who wish to earn a living for themselves and their families.

Significantly, the late Frederick Hayek, Nobel Laureate, made exactly the same point when he wrote about U.S. Labor Law,

> It cannot be stressed enough that the coercion which unions have been permitted to exercise contrary to all principles of freedom under the law is primarily the coercion of fellow workers. Whatever true coercive power unions may be able to wield over employers is a consequence of this primary power of coercing other workers; the coercion of employees would lose most of its objectionable character if unions were deprived of this power to exact unwilling support.

Checking the Power of Union Officials

However, there is no evidence that unions based on this "enforced" solidarity are more valuable to working people and to the country than those based on principles of freedom. In fact, it was President Kennedy's Secretary of Labor, Arthur Goldberg, a former union lawyer, who told a union audience in Washington in 1962 that "very often even the union that has won the union shop will frankly admit that people who come in through that route do not always participate in the same knowing way as people who come in through the method of education and voluntarism."

The late Supreme Court Justice Louis Brandeis probably summarized this principle best when he said,

> The union attains success when it reaches the ideal condition. And the ideal condition for a union is to be strong and stable and yet to have in the trade outside its own ranks an appreciable number of men who are non-unionists. Such a nucleus of unorganized labor will check oppression by the union as the union checks oppression by the employer.

Too often, union officials are more driven to maintain their coercive privileges than to win wage and benefit increases for the employees they claim to represent. Let me cite an example.

In March, 1994, A.B. Hirschfeld Press ended the practice of forcing its employees to pay union dues. One month later, the Denver local of the Graphic Communications Union began a strike in which the forced-dues payments were the only issue. In fact, Local 440's Secretary-Treasurer admitted to *The Denver Post* that the union hierarchy was willing to "accept a pact in which workers would have had their wages frozen" but was "adamant that it never will accept Hirschfeld's demand for an 'open shop.'"

Although this injustice—the pressure on employers to barter away employee freedom in exchange for dollar benefits for themselves—is a common occurrence, it rarely comes into public view. The particular incident cited here came to light only because union officials were threatening to boycott a Democratic fundraising event featuring Mrs. Gore, the Vice-President's wife, and co-sponsored by the plant owner's wife.

Many employers are unwilling—or unable—to endure the costs of protracted and violent strikes to protect their employees from forced union membership. It should come as no surprise that some employers will leap at the union bosses' offer of lower wages and fewer benefits for the employees if the employer will simply hand them over to the union.

Using their government-granted coercive power, union officials collected nearly $5 billion in forced-union dues from private sector workers alone in 1999. And as the Steelworkers union admitted in their own newsletter, these forced dues seized by local union bosses across the country "can't go for direct political contributions—but it can do a lot: mailings supporting or opposing candidates, phone banks, precinct visits, voter registration and get-out-the-vote drives."

Testifying before the U.S. Senate less than one month ago, Rutgers University economist Leo Troy estimated that Big Labor spends well over $300 million on "in-kind" political activities during every two-year election cycle—and that's just the money they spend on Federal elections.

The Rank and File Do Not Benefit

Indeed, it is high time that we go directly to the heart of the matter—the merits or demerits of the Congressional sanction of compulsory unionism. This is the real issue—should union membership be voluntary or compulsory? The underlying philosophy of those who believe in the Right to Work principle can be best summed up in the words of Samuel Gompers, founder of the American Federation of Labor, who urged "devotion to the fundaments of human liberty— the principles of voluntarism. No lasting gain has ever come from compulsion. If we seek to force, we but tear apart that which, united, is invincible."

The most perceptive observers, both inside and outside Organized Labor, have long recognized that compulsory membership in unions is not necessarily beneficial to the rank and file employee whose interest the union is supposed to serve. In fact, some of the most dedicated advocates of Organized Labor have concluded that the best interest of the labor movement itself is hurt more than it is helped by reliance upon compulsion in attracting and retaining members.

In fact, Donald Richberg, author of the Railway Labor Act, top advisor to the Roosevelt Administration, and a lifelong, active friend of Organized Labor, could only lament: "It is hard to understand how labor unions, which have developed voluntary organizations of self-help to free labor from any oppression of employer power, can justify their present program of using the employer's control of jobs to force men into unions to which they do not wish to belong."

Upholding the Right to Work

Unfortunately, as the union movement has evolved from the Gompers era of dedicated leadership to the present-day era of a giant union "establishment," characterized by high-salaried and highly privileged professional union officials, the attitude toward forced membership has hardened into one of total opposition to all forms of voluntarism. In the lexicon of today's union boss, Right to Work legislation or voluntary unionism is a dirty word. They have invested millions and millions of forced-dues dollars in campaigns to convince the public that Right to Work laws and anti-unionism are synonymous. Many politicians have mistaken the shrill voice of union-financed propaganda for the voice of the worker himself. . . .

The Right to Work movement is a coalition of employees and employers who speak for *all* Americans who believe in voluntary rather than compulsory membership. Every citizen has a stake in restoring conditions which will lead to responsibility and responsiveness on the part of union leadership. Compulsory unionism sets the stage for most of the abuses of union power—abuses which work to the detriment of all segments of the American public.

Over the years, employer groups have sought to treat the symptoms—to correct abuses growing out of compulsory unionism—rather than attacking the root of the problem. Laws have placed certain restrictions over the internal affairs of unions: control of union elections, licensing of union officials, publication of union financial records and many more. Other than creating complex administrative machinery, these efforts have had little or no effect on the real problem.

D. Cooper for *The People*; © Socialist Labor Party. Used with permission.

We believe that labor legislation should adhere to a policy of providing true freedom of choice for the worker—that given a choice he will *insist* on responsible union leadership. And I believe that *responsible* union leaders should welcome Right to Work. Union leaders who truly seek to represent the interests of employees would surely agree with the late Senator Sam Ervin, who once wrote that "right-to-work laws remove the motive of the union to subordinate the interests of the employees to its wish, and thus leave it free to conduct negotiations for the sole purpose of obtaining a contract advantageous to the employees."

In fact, some union leaders do now understand, albeit

grudgingly. In 1996, in Lynchburg, Virginia, a local Steel-workers official told the *Daily Advance*, "It's a strange thing about a right-to-work state. . . . We get 100 percent participation during contract negotiations."

After Idaho voters approved a Right to Work referendum in 1986, Idaho's American Federation of Labor–Congress of Industrial Organizations (AFL-CIO) chief admitted that union organizers would "have to learn something about contacting the worker and asking him to join, *which they haven't had a great amount of experience in.*"

And having failed to repeal Tennessee's Right to Work law, the AFL-CIO now must, in the words of AFL-CIO executive vice president Linda Chavez-Thompson, "go out into those communities and show (non-members) that we are also members of those communities." Maybe then, Chavez-Thompson speculates, "*they will want to join unions.*" Exactly!

In 1996, Fred Comer, Executive Director of the teachers union in Iowa, the affiliate of the National Education Association (NEA), commented on the NEA's highly controversial action calling for a nationwide "homosexuality awareness month" in all the public schools. Comer was asked if his Iowa NEA affiliate would support that program. His response: ". . . No we don't support it. Iowa is a Right to Work state, we have to earn our membership. If we supported that, we'd lose too many members."

Unfortunately, the new AFL-CIO hierarchy seems bent on such "innovative" techniques of increasing their membership as blocking roads during rush hour and so-called "corporate campaigns" designed to force employers to deliver their employees over to the union without so much as a secret vote.

Majority Support for Voluntary Unionism

I bear little hope that AFL-CIO chief John Sweeney and his lieutenant, Richard Trumka, will heed the nearly 60 percent of *union* members who, according to scientific polling, oppose forced unionism propped up by Federal law. I am more hopeful that you and the rest of the U.S. Congress will heed those union members shouting, "I want my union back."

If that isn't enough, I implore this subcommittee to listen

to the nearly 80 percent of *all* Americans who support giving all employees the Right to Work regardless of whether or not they pay union dues.

The National Right to Work Act presents the United States House of Representatives with the clearest of choices as to the focus on Federal labor policy for the new millennium. On one side stand the American people who have declared in every credible poll their overwhelming opposition to compulsory unionism.

On the other side stands the AFL-CIO hierarchy and its allies in the House, who have used any and all means to preserve the forced-dues provisions in Federal law.

I ask the members of this subcommittee to side with the American people and begin the process of ending compulsory unionism.

Thank you for the opportunity to address this urgent matter.

> "*The most a union may require is that the worker pay a pro-rated share of that portion of the union dues and initiation fees that are used for collective bargaining, contract administration or grievance adjustment.*"

Requiring Workers to Pay Union Fees Is Fair

William L. Clay

William L. Clay argues in the following viewpoint that requiring union dues from all employees in unionized workplaces is a fair practice that permits the majority of workers who desire union representation to effectively bargain to improve their economic status. Right-to-work laws which preclude employees from having to pay dues to a union, merely serve corporate interests by financially weakening unions and undermining their bargaining power, in the author's opinion. This in turn contributes to lower wages and increased rates of poverty and unemployment. Clay is a former Democratic congressman from Missouri who served on the House Education and the Workforce Committee.

As you read, consider the following questions:

1. How do right-to-work laws undermine the cohesion of unions, in Clay's opinion?
2. According to the author, what is the most that a union may require of a worker in states without right-to-work laws?
3. What remedies does Clay suggest are available to workers dissatisfied with their union representation?

Excerpted from "Does America Need a National Right-to-Work Law? No," by William L. Clay, *Insight on the News*, August 17, 1998. Copyright © 1998 by News World Communications. Reprinted with permission.

The late Rev. Martin Luther King Jr. probably said it best when he proclaimed: "In our glorious fight for civil rights, we must guard against being fooled by false slogans, as 'right to work.' It provides no 'rights' and no 'works.' Its purpose is to destroy labor unions and the freedom of collective bargaining."

Corporate interests and their allies consistently contend that "right-to-work" laws create jobs or protect individual liberties. So-called right-to-work laws do nothing of the sort. In fact, if we are to be accurate, such laws should be referred to as "right-to-work-for-less laws." Right-to-work-for-less laws are all about weakening and destroying unions—institutions created by and for workers for the express purpose of protecting the rights of workers on and off the job.

A right-to-work-for-less law does not create a single job. Nor does it provide workers with any meaningful employment rights. What right-to-work-for-less laws do produce is lower pay and harder times for workers and their families. A right-to-work-for-less law is an antidemocratic loophole created in 1947 by a Republican Congress. Such laws permit states to effectively amend federal law to prohibit unions from being able to charge for the services they provide to workers.

Right-to-work-for-less laws provide that no worker may be required to pay the union for its services, even though the law requires unions to represent all workers fairly in the bargaining unit (dues payers and nondues payers alike). The law holds unions fully liable for failing to meet those responsibilities.

In effect, right-to-work-for-less laws destroy the financial underpinning of unions by permitting some workers to be free riders and enjoy the benefits of union representation while refusing to pay their fair share for union services. This is true even though the union would not exist if it was not desired by a majority of the workers.

Right-to-work-for-less laws also undermine the cohesion of unions. While the union works for the benefit of all workers, right-to-work-for-less laws permit some workers to refuse to pay any of the costs associated with the attainment of those benefits. As a result, other workers are forced to pay more than their fair share and, understandably, they will tend to resent the workers who they are forced to subsidize.

The detrimental impact that right-to-work-for-less laws have on the rights and standard of living for workers is obvious. In 1995, the American Federation of Labor and Congress of Industrial Organizations (AFL-CIO) compiled a statistical comparison of states with right-to-work-for-less laws vs. states without such laws. Workers in states without right-to-work-for-less laws made an average of $4,343, or 18 percent more annually than workers in states with right-to-work-for-less laws. Significantly, not a single one of 21 states that have enacted right-to-work-for-less laws had a pay level above the national average. Weekly paychecks for production workers in states without right-to-work-for-less laws averaged $68.56, or 16 percent higher. Personal income broke down as follows:

Average Incomes:

All States	$20,781
States without right-to-work-for-less laws	$21,829
Right-to-work states	$18,873

The negative impact of right-to-work-for-less laws extends far beyond a worker's paycheck. The percentage of the population living below the poverty line was greater than the national average in states with right-to-work-for-less laws. School-dropout rates were higher than the national average in states with right-to-work-for-less laws. In addition, states with right-to-work-for-less laws have higher infant-mortality rates and a higher percentage of people without health insurance.

Unemployment and workers'-compensation benefits were substantially lower for workers in right-to-work-for-less states than in other states, while instances of business bankruptcies were higher in right-to-work-for-less states. Right-to-work-for-less states were far more dependent upon regressive sales taxes that unfairly take a higher portion of income from workers than from the wealthy. At the same time, right-to-work-for-less states spent less in per-pupil school expenditures. Right-to-work-for-less laws do not simply undermine the ability of workers to be able to negotiate terms and conditions of employment, they undermine the influence and rights of workers throughout society. In summary, right-to-work-for-less laws result in lower pay, fewer work-based benefits, increased poverty, diminished health-care protections, higher bankruptcy rates, regressive taxes and a decreased emphasis on investment in education. Quite a record of achievement!

Corporate Backing of Anti-Unionism

The anti-union roots of "right-to-work" run deep. The National Association of Manufacturers originally started the anti-union, open shop movement in 1905 to combat unions. Later during the 1920s and 1930s, it became known as the "American Plan," an aggressive employer effort to stamp out unions.

The modern "right-to-work" movement was started by southern business leaders who for years tried to hide their corporate backing. Today the main front group is a right-wing organization called the National Right to Work Committee (NRTWC) which is funded and controlled by anti-union business executives.

A court suit brought against the Committee revealed that more than 80 percent of its contributions come from business and corporate sources. Headquartered in Virginia since the early 1990s, the NRTWC and its legal foundation receive annual contributions of more than $9 million to fight and harass unions.

More insidious is the often overlooked racial underside of "right-to-work." For minorities, union membership has always presented a path to economic and social empowerment. The NRTWC was born out of the segregated South by wealthy white business leaders who wanted to prevent the spread of unionism.

Martin Maddaloni, *AIL Labor Agenda*, March 1999.

President Harry S. Truman observed, "You will find some people saying that they are for the so-called 'right-to-work' law, but they also believe in unions. This is absurd—it's like saying you are for motherhood but against children."

Unions are organizations formed of workers, by workers, for workers. To form unions, workers must demonstrate that the majority of workers who would be represented by the union desire that representation. Even where a union is established, employers cannot give preference to union members in hiring workers nor can any employee be required to join the union. Workers can refuse to attend union meetings, they may refuse to support strikes and they are free to resign union membership, all without fear of being fired by their employer. Workers even may engage in wildcat strikes without fear of union punishment, though the union itself consequently may be subject to damages. At regular intervals, a majority of employees may vote out the union or choose another in its place.

In states that have not enacted right-to-work-for-less laws, the most a union may require is that the worker pay a pro-rated share of that portion of the union dues and initiation fees that are used for collective bargaining, contract administration or grievance adjustment. Typically, workers cannot be required to pay that until after the first 30 days of employment.

Unions, by law, must be operated in accordance with democratic principles. It is the workers who decide how much their dues will be and how the money will be used. However, by law, union dues may not be excessive nor may they be discriminatory. Typically, union dues are equal to the equivalent of two hours of wages, but no employee is required to either join the union or pay full union dues. Further, unions must inform employees that they are not required to pay full union dues. They must inform employees of the percentage of union dues that are used for purposes other than collective bargaining, contract administration or grievance adjustment. Those who choose not to join the union cannot be required to pay money that is used for other purposes, including purposes that are integral to the functioning of the union such as organizing and litigation. No employee can be required as a condition of employment to pay any money that is used by a union for political activities.

The law already fully and appropriately balances the interests of the majority of workers desiring union representation and the minority who do not. To the extent that a worker is dissatisfied with a union, he or she has democratically protected rights to work within the union to change its policies or officers. In addition, a worker may work democratically with fellow workers to decertify the union or replace it with another. The worker may choose not to be a member of the union and to refuse to underwrite any of the union's activities that are not directly related to the provision of representational services at the workplace. Finally, the worker has a right to work democratically to persuade the voters of the worker's state to enact a right-to-work-for-less law.

In the view of those who would destroy the fight of workers to bargain collectively, however, it is not enough that states, despite the harm it causes, may enact their own right-to-work-for-less laws if they so choose. In their view, we should impose such laws on all states; they are lobbying Congress, as is their right, to do so. They will not succeed soon. [Former] House Speaker Newt Gingrich has said that such legislation, "does not have the support necessary to pass in the House, and it would be foolish to schedule a vote that is sure to fail."

For the vast majority of workers in this country, the contemporary economic environment renders it impossible for workers to improve their economic status through individual bargaining. Rather, to have an effective voice in the determination of their wages and benefits and the establishment of terms and conditions of employment, many workers have found it necessary to band together and bargain collectively. Where employees have chosen to form unions and have persevered through the employer opposition that often accompanies that decision, they have succeeded in improving both their own living standards and those of everyone else.

Unions are an integral part of the political process that has made possible the 40-hour workweek, the minimum wage and Social Security. Unions, acting for those they represent, were responsible for establishing pension and health-benefit plans that now are a feature of many nonunion, as well as union, compensation plans. Unions play an invaluable role in ensuring that all Americans have an opportunity to benefit in the richest economy and freest society in the world. Sadly, despite the booming economy of the Clinton era, studies indicate that the gap between the richest and poorest in our country is increasing. Without question, existing state right-to-work-for-less laws have exacerbated this problem. Unless we desire a country in which only a few benefit from the wealth we produce while everyone else struggles just to make ends meet, we do not need a national right-to-work-for-less law.

"Today's unions are working to secure important rights and benefits for contingent workers."

Contingent Workers Will Benefit from Union Representation

John J. Sweeney

Throughout the 1990s, the use of temporary, part-time, and contract employees—collectively referred to as "contingent" workers—continued to grow rapidly as companies sought to cut costs through the use of a more flexible workforce. In the following viewpoint, John J. Sweeney argues that unscrupulous employers often exploit contingent workers by paying them lower wages and benefits than those paid to permanent employees. Therefore, contingent workers will benefit from the higher pay and legal advocacy that union representation provides, in the author's opinion. Sweeney is president of the American Federation of Labor–Congress of Industrial Organizations (AFL-CIO), the voluntary federation of unions representing more than 13 million workers nationwide.

As you read, consider the following questions:

1. According to Sweeney, what does the General Accounting Office report on contingent employment confirm about the "employment relationship"?
2. How do contingent workers fall through the cracks of the nation's worker protection and benefits safety net, in the author's opinion?

Reprinted, with permission, from "Statement by John J. Sweeney, AFL-CIO President, on the New GAO Report Shows Contingent Worker Incomes and Benefits Lag," AFL-CIO news release, July 26, 2000, at www.aflcio.org/publ/press2000/pr0726.htm.

On July 26, 2000, the General Accounting Office (GAO) released its report on the current status of the 30 percent of the workforce in "contingent" or "non-standard" employment arrangements.

The GAO's discussion of these independent contractors and workers in part-time, temporary and contract jobs, "Contingent Workers: Incomes and Benefits Lag Behind Those of Rest of Workforce," helps sharpen our understanding of non-standard employment, its magnitude and some of its consequences, and the need for sensitive, sensible and creative responses to the challenges and opportunities these arrangements present for working families.

The Growth of a Contingent Workforce

The report confirms that for millions of workers, there has been a fundamental and substantial shift in the employment relationship away from long-term, stable employment with a single employer, toward less secure, often intermittent work for multiple firms.

Non-standard work is not confined to one group of workers or one region. White collar, blue collar, pink collar, no collar; from high tech West Coast "permatemps" to day laborers in Atlanta; in every industry, in unionized and unorganized workplaces alike, contingent workers are a core part of the workforce. And, contrary to earlier experience, non-standard work is not a response to an economy in disarray. Instead, it has persisted *despite* a strong recovery and is an institutionalized feature of the economy and of most employers' workforces.

In a recent American Management Association survey, nearly all firms (93 percent) said they hire contingent workers, and half (49 percent) use more such workers now than in 1996. Two-thirds (65 percent) of firms in a 1996 Upjohn Institute survey said employers will likely hire more contingent workers in the future.

Work Without Protections and Benefits

Non-standard work is a matter of choice for some workers: many—though not all—well educated and well paid independent contractors enjoy the autonomy of self-employment;

many part-timers elect shorter workweeks to accommodate family or other demands.

For millions of non-standard workers, however, temporary, contract or part-time work is *not* a choice: it is their only option. And for some—chicken catchers working for poultry magnate Frank Perdue, for example, or construction workers intentionally misclassified as independent contractors instead of employees—non-standard work is a status their employers unilaterally and unlawfully impose upon them in order to deny them protections and benefits.

Regardless of the reasons individuals are in non-standard jobs, the status has real and significant consequences for most workers. Most are paid less than similarly skilled regular full-time employees, even when they do the same work for the same employer. Non-standard workers are also less likely—and low income non-standard workers, much less likely—than regular employees to have employer-provided health insurance and pension coverage. Non-standard workers are frequently unable to collect unemployment benefits when out of work because eligibility rules in many states either expressly exclude them or have the effect of doing so.

Equally serious, non-standard workers often fall outside or through the cracks of the nation's worker protection and benefits safety net. For example, because they are not "employees," independent contractors have few federally protected rights, including minimum wage and overtime pay protections or the right to organize and bargain collectively.

Laws that cover only those workers who meet certain hourly or weekly thresholds of employment each year—the Family and Medical Leave Act and the Employee Retirement Income Security Act, among others—exclude many temporary and part-time employees. And workers employed by one company (an intermediary firm, such as a temp agency or a contract company) to work for another (a client company) often have few or no rights and remedies against the client company, because the courts consider them to be employees only of the intermediary firm.

The American Federation of Labor–Congress of Industrial Organizations (AFL-CIO) and its affiliate unions are committed to ending exploitation and abuse of contingent workers: through (1) more aggressive enforcement of existing laws where unscrupulous employers deliberately misclassify workers in order to deny them their rights, and (2) advocacy for new laws and policies that guarantee equal rights and fair treatment—an end to second class status—for contingent workers.

We know that a worker protection safety net that provides uneven and uncertain safeguards for three of every 10 workers must be fixed. That's why we support measures such as the proposed Employee Benefits Eligibility Fairness Act of 2000, which would prohibit employers from denying workers benefits by misclassifying them; and H.R. 1525, the Independent Contractor Clarification Act, which would simplify and clarify the tax code test to determine whether an individual is an employee or a contractor.

The union movement is also committed to helping contingent workers win a voice at work. Today's unions are working to secure important rights and benefits for contingent workers through traditional organizing, bargaining, and collective activity, *and* through new and innovative initiatives designed to provide representation and benefits for independent contractors and other self-employed workers who truly prefer to operate autonomously but who nevertheless need the protections that a union provides.

Successful Organizing

The Teamsters struck United Parcel Service (UPS), demanding higher pay, better benefits, and new guarantees of full-time employment for part-time workers. The building trades unions of the AFL-CIO have launched a national campaign highlighting abuses of temporary employment in the construction industry and have begun organizing temp workers to help them win a voice at work. In July 2000, the Atlanta Building Trades Council joined forces with day laborers who are suing Labor Ready over the company's policy of deducting a fee, ranging from $1.00 to $1.99, from workers when they redeem their day's cash wages from the company's cash dispensing machines.

The United Food and Commercial Workers Union bargains strong benefits packages for its members in part-time

Temps Turn to Unions

Amid Silicon Valley's torrid dot-com boom, stories abound of peach-fuzzed college graduates pulling down six-figure salaries and, in short order, securing their American dream. For them there is no shortage of opportunity—for new business ventures, luxury cars and seven-figure homes. Yet beneath this gilded veneer a class war is brewing. The Valley's legions of temps dream of getting full-time jobs and keeping homelessness at bay in a place where the median home price has soared to $365,000 and a standard two-bedroom apartment rents for $1,500 a month.

For veteran Silicon Valley temp workers like Julian Cornejo, the stark disparities drive home the point that temps—long underpaid, underemployed and "disposable"—must band together to improve conditions and restrict the ability of employers to exploit their labor. Cornejo's experience illustrates the precariousness of the contingent life. A mechanical designer with thirty years' experience, he has been stuck on the temp-work treadmill, with no benefits or job security, for fifteen years. After suffering a shoulder injury while temping at a Palo Alto semiconductor firm in 1998, Cornejo spent nearly a year fighting his temp agency for workers' compensation, leaving him broke and in debt.

Fed up with the powerlessness and isolation, in February 1999 Cornejo went looking for a temp labor union. What he found, thanks to a story in a local newspaper, was a unique temp workers' association called Working Partnerships USA. Launched by San Jose's South Bay AFL-CIO Labor Council in 1995, Working Partnerships runs a nonprofit temp firm and offers health insurance for temps. Emphasizing membership services, it occupies one end of a spectrum of new organizations for contingent workers, rising up both within and outside unions, that are giving voice and structure to a growing chorus of temp-worker frustrations. As Eileen Wodjula, a Working Partnerships member and Silicon Valley temp for several years, puts it, "We have to start all over again, with a new workers' movement."

Christopher D. Cook, *Nation*, March 27, 2000.

jobs and, just recently, won a voice at work for chicken catchers working for Perdue Farms in Delaware and Maryland. Through its Justice for Janitors campaign, the Service Employees International Union represents tens of thousands of low paid janitors working for building service contractors in major cities around the nation and has successfully negotiated new contracts covering roughly 100,000 workers. In 1999, 75,000 home care workers in Los Angeles County, a group of mostly low paid women of color, once classified as independent contractors, won their voice at work—and a first contract—when they voted "yes" to representation by the Service Employees International Union.

The Communications Workers of America (CWA) successfully negotiated creation of an "Administrative Intern" program at AT&T facilities in New Jersey in response to the company's growing reliance on temporary workers. Though Administrative Interns rotate among departments and assignments, they are covered under the collective bargaining agreement and receive good union wages, benefits and other protections. Similarly, the American Federation of State, County and Municipal Employees (AFSCME) Council 13 and Pennsylvania created an internal public sector temporary worker pool, providing the state with the flexibility it felt it needed to meet temporary needs while preserving public jobs and enhancing protections for temporary workers.

New Models of Representation

Unions are also developing new models of representation for contingent workers who, by choice or otherwise, will likely continue to fall outside of the traditional employer-employee relationship. In 1999, the New York State Psychological Association, a membership association of about 3300 mostly self-employed psychologists, affiliated with the New York State United Teachers and the American Federation of Teachers (AFT). The unions and the association will join forces to advocate legal reforms designed to curb managed care abuse and protect professional standards; they are also exploring strategies for providing benefits to the association's members. In addition, the AFT is collaborating with Working Today to explore the development of a portable benefits program for part-time and self-employed professionals.

In Washington State, CWA has chartered a new local, WashTech, an organization of high tech workers formed in the wake of the successful "permatemp" litigation against Microsoft. In addition to organizing to win a voice at work for high tech employees, WashTech and CWA are lobbying to secure greater protections for all high tech workers, regardless of their classification, and are exploring strategies for providing benefits and bargaining on behalf of agency employees. AFSCME and the Office and Professional Employees International Union are organizing among self-employed doctors and dentists in several states.

In San Jose, the South Bay Central Labor Council and Working Partnerships USA have established Together@Work, a labor-led temporary employment agency that aims to raise standards for temporary employment in the Valley, thus affecting industry practices, raising the wage floor for low wage earners, and providing greater employment stability. Together@Work temps earn higher hourly wages than other agencies' temps *and* they receive pension, health benefits, and training. To ensure quality, Together@Work meets regional skills standards prescribed by an employer advisory council.

Through these and other strategies, the union movement is fighting to extend full and fair benefits, rights and protections to all workers, regardless of their status. Working families don't lead contingent lives—and neither should their rights and protections on the job and their opportunity to receive good wages and benefits be contingent on their status as permanent or full-time employees.

"Workplace regulations and union shops . . . represent costly intrusions to the workplace."

Contingent Workers Will Not Benefit from Union Representation

Christopher Westley

Temporary employees, along with part-time and contract workers, make up the "contingent" workforce, which encompasses 30 percent of U.S. workers. The use of temporary employees doubled in the 1990s as employers attempted to circumvent costly union regulations regarding the hiring, wages, and benefits of permanent, full-time employees. Christopher Westley maintains in the following viewpoint that efforts to unionize temporary workers will hurt the U.S. economy by reducing employer flexibility in the management of workforces. Unionization of temporary workers is destined to fail and will only entangle the labor market in more regulations, in the author's opinion. Westley teaches economics at Jacksonville State University in Jacksonville, Alabama.

As you read, consider the following questions:
1. How do unions cause employers to lose labor flexibility, in the author's opinion?
2. According to Westley, why do companies using temporary workers find it easier to fire non-productive workers as opposed to those using union workers?
3. Why will the unionization of temporary workers fail, in Westley's opinion?

Reprinted, with permission, from "Unionizing Temps," by Christopher Westley, posted on the Ludwig von Mises Institute website, www.mises.org/fullarticle.asp?record=498&month=24, September 2, 2000.

The National Labor Relations Board (NLRB) is the Supreme Soviet of organized labor. Created by [former President] Franklin Delano Roosevelt to impose unions on the American workforce, its abolishment is long overdue. Instead, it is attempting to impose union membership on the very sector of the labor force that has appeal primarily because of its freedom from union influence.

This sector is the temp industry which, as a percentage of the workforce, doubled in size in the 1990s. In fact, it is not well known that the largest private employer in the U.S. is no longer General Motors, a title it relinquished in the early 1990s. The largest employer, hands down, is a Milwaukee-based temp agency that is called Manpower.

Unions and Regulations Fuel Temp Industry

It's likely that either you have worked for Manpower or know someone who has. The increasing significance of temporary workers in our economy is directly related to the rise of workplace regulations and union shops, which represent costly intrusions to the workplace that hamper business productivity while expanding the state. The temp industry is a major reason why the economy grew so much in the 1990s.

This intervention into the workplace means that employers have fewer options at their disposal when market conditions suggest a change in the make-up of its labor pool is in order. It rewards them for using capital-intensive production techniques when labor-intensive production might have been just as feasible. The loss in labor flexibility means that employers are less able to take advantage of profit opportunities that arise when market conditions call for increased production of goods. The loss in flexibility also means that employers are less able to scale back their workforces when reduced production is called for as well.

Such a situation benefits large firms because it increases the cost to smaller competitors. Indeed, it reduces the degree of competition and entrepreneurial activity in general because the regulatory framework is biased toward the big, established firms that can afford to comply with the costs.

That is why understanding temp agencies is crucial to understanding the economic growth of the 1990s, a decade that began with massive regulatory legislation during the Bush Administration, especially in the form of the Civil Rights Act of 1990 and the Americans with Disabilities Act. Employers were able to opt out of complying with these pieces of regulation, to the extent that they affected the size and composition of their labor pools, by hiring temp workers. Firms that needed to reduce production simply give the temp workers back to firms like Manpower. These workers' labor resources are then employed at other firms that demand it, improving economic efficiency and labor flexibility.

Low-Cost Labor a Threat to Unions

These employers didn't have to worry about potential lawsuits if the worker proved to be a poor one and needed to be dismissed. After all, the employee was actually employed by the temp agency, so if he didn't work out, he could be dismissed by the firm, for whatever reason. Imagine that!

The unions, and their cronies at the NLRB, have been doing more than imagining this phenomenon. They witness it, up close and personal, often in their own workplaces. And they don't like it.

The ability to fire non-productive workers at will may be a boon to firms competing in global markets, and it may be a boon to consumers who have access to more products at lower prices, but it is a bust to union workers. The existence of mobile, low-cost labor gaining access to the unionized segment of the labor force threatens the very future of organized labor.

The proper way to think of organized labor is as a labor cartel. In fact, it was amusing to read about unionized truckers protesting OPEC when gas prices surged as a result of its temporary success in reducing world oil production. Cartels can be effective only when they are successful at reducing output and restricting entry—which is impossible to achieve in the long run under free market conditions. Those union workers benefited from the same industrial organization as did OPEC's member countries, except that while one group's product was oil, the other's was labor.

The primary difference between the two is that when OPEC forces an increase in world oil prices, it causes entrepreneurs to shift their resources toward oil production. As a result, its cartel cannot remain effective, so long as government policy doesn't impede the process. This is known as the Law of Supply in economics, which states that rising prices signal to producers which resources should be employed.

Tampering with Temps Will Increase Unemployment

Temporary help employment is not common, and long-term temporary help employees are even more rare. Temporary help employees with more than 24 months of tenure—about 170,000 workers—constitute about 0.1 percent of the work-force. Given the fact that there are over a million temporary help employees currently, and many more work in temp jobs at some point during the course of a year, the number of long-term temps is remarkably low. Moreover, these long-term temporary help employees are more likely than other temps to be in "good" temporary jobs—jobs that they prefer, that pay well and offer employment benefits.

Proposals to restrict the use of temporary help employment appear regularly. Illinois representative Lane Evans intro-duced two bills that would "require employers to offer tem-porary workers the same benefits they provide their full-time, permanent workforce, [and] bar discrimination against temporary help workers in rates of pay. . . ." Proposals such as these all share one feature—they would reduce the num-ber of temporary help jobs available to workers. These poli-cies are misguided for at least two reasons. First, . . . there are very few individuals who involuntarily "wind up" in tempo-rary help employment for any appreciable length of time. Second, the alternative to temping is not necessarily tradi-tional employment for many individuals. Many of those who would be dislocated from temporary jobs as a result of leg-islative changes would become unemployed rather than find alternate employment.

To the extent that long-term involuntary temporary help employment is viewed as a problem, policies that ensure workers have adequate workplace skills are more likely to benefit both workers and employers.

Employment Policy Foundation, "Long-Term Temps: A Rare Breed," *Backgrounder*, 1999.

When unions force an increase in wage rates by controlling the labor supply, they also attract nonunion labor resources to the unionized industry, because a wage is simply the price of labor services. Under normal conditions, this response would force nominal wages and prices down, but normal conditions are not optimal for the unions' survival. Fueled largely by union soft money donations, the government intervenes in this process, introducing much legal and physical force that is necessary whenever voluntary exchange is restricted.

Unionizing Temps Won't Work

Temp agencies represent the most recent attempt by employers and employees to circumvent this situation, which has troubled the NLRB commissars. So in August 2000, predictably, the NLRB voted to remove restrictions on unionizing temp workers, a move that, if successful, would remove the benefits from using these workers in the first place. Their appeal as a legal way around interventions in the workplace would be lost. Former NLRB board member John Raudabaugh admitted as much when he said, "I think this will cause people to reassess whether they're going to use temporary help."

Talk about an understatement. Actually, the NLRB's decision, which could be overruled by an executive order from the president, reflects a growing trend by the non-productive to impose the very institutional arrangements that impair their performance on the productive. After all, isn't this a primary purpose of the World Trade Organization—to insure that regulations are equally imposed and adhered to by all member countries? In a nutshell, this is all the NLRB is trying to do. It is trying to remove the advantage that temp labor has over union labor.

It won't work. Employers will dismiss most temp workers who join the union forthwith, giving them little incentive to join the union shops. This, no doubt, will produce even more regulation in the future, requiring employers to prove that union-joining temp workers were dismissed for reasons other than their union membership. The added regulations make for an administrative law judge's dream.

If only the NLRB was a part of the temp sector and not the government sector, we could give it back to temp firms like Manpower.

Periodical Bibliography

The following articles have been selected to supplement the diverse views presented in this chapter. Addresses are provided for periodicals not indexed in the *Readers' Guide to Periodical Literature*, the *Alternative Press Index*, the *Social Sciences Index*, or the *Index to Legal Periodicals and Books*.

James T. Bennett	"Right to Work—Prescription for Prosperity," National Institute for Labor Relations Research, n.d. Website: www.nilrr.org/histandard.htm.
Aaron Bernstein	"Labor Is Growing Again—but Not Without Some Pain," *Businessweek Online*, January 19, 2000. Website: www.businessweek.com.
Christopher D. Cook	"Temps Demand a New Deal," *Nation*, March 27, 2000.
Tim Costello and S.M. Miller	"Rethinking Labor," *Social Policy*, Winter 1998.
The Economist	"Mother Jones Meets the Microchip," June 12, 1999.
Mark Fitzgerald	"Guild Targets Microsoft," *Editor & Publisher*, January 30, 1999.
Samuel Francis	"Big Business and Big Labor Vs. the Workers," *Wanderer*, August 27, 1998.
Steven Greenhouse	"Labor Board Makes Union Membership Easier for Temps," *New York Times*, August 31, 2000.
Steven Greenhouse	"Union Leaders See Grim News in Labor Study," *New York Times*, October 13, 1999.
Carrie Johnson	"@Work; Ruling on Temps Reflects a Changing Workplace," *Washington Post*, September 10, 2000.
Margret Johnston	"Unions See a Role for Themselves in New Economy," *Network World*, December 4, 2000.
Julie Kosterlitz	"Searching for New Labor," *National Journal*, September 4, 1999.
Reed Larson	"Time to End Compulsory Unionism," *Wall Street Journal*, February 26, 1997.
Joshua Micah Marshall	"Payback Time," *American Prospect*, April 9, 2001.
David Moberg	"Union Cities," *American Prospect*, September 11, 2000.

Neil Munro   "Class Struggle in Silicon Valley," *National Journal*, September 4, 1999.

Joseph Perkins   "Union Workers Want to Protect Their Paychecks," *San Diego Union-Tribune*, April 24, 1998.

Steve Proffitt   "Amy Dean: Labor Plugs in to the Uncertain Lives of Knowledge Workers," *Los Angeles Times*, October 10, 1999.

Howard D. Samuel   "Troubled Passage: The Labor Movement and the Fair Labor Standards Act," *Monthly Labor Review*, December 2000.

Leo Troy   "The UPS Strike: Labor Tilts at Windmills," *Heritage Foundation Backgrounder*, March 23, 1998.

David Wagner   "Big Labor Fights a Losing Battle," *Insight on the News*, May 18, 1998.

CHAPTER 4

How Should Equality in the Workplace Be Achieved?

Chapter Preface

Since the early efforts of the women's movement to eradicate gender discrimination from the American workplace in the 1960s, women have made important advances in their rates of participation in the workforce. Three out of four women between the ages of 20–54 are now working, according to the U.S. Department of Labor's Women's Bureau.

Despite these gains, many observers contend that wage discrimination rewards occupations traditionally dominated by women, such as nursing, with lower wages than occupations requiring comparable skills and education dominated by men, such as fireman. Advocates for ending wage discrimination assert that "comparable worth" policies are the answer to this gender wage gap. These policies, enacted in several U.S. states, mandate that men and women working different jobs requiring comparable skills and education receive the same wages. Explains Karen Nussbaum of the American Federation of Labor-Congress of Industrial Organizations (AFL-CIO), "It is illegal to pay women less than men in the same job . . . [but] most women are not covered because they're in female-dominated jobs. . . . [Comparable worth] laws would strengthen enforcement and expand the notion of equal pay to work of equal value."

Critics of comparable worth policies argue that women earn less on average than men as a result of educational and career choices. According to Dominique Lazanski, a public policy fellow at the Pacific Research Institute, "Historically, more women have pursued degrees in less financially rewarding fields of study than [men] . . . while accumulating less continuous time in the workforce. . . . Each of these factors bears directly on position and compensation levels." Others contend that enacting comparative worth laws will hurt female job-seekers. Says Anita Hattiangadi, an economist at the Employment Policy Foundation, "Increased employer cost would reduce job opportunities for women."

Pay equity for women is one area where equality in the workplace is in question. The authors in the following chapter debate this topic along with the employment rights of minority and disabled workers.

"Affirmative action programs actually do work [without] . . . creating barriers to employment of white males."

Affirmative Action Promotes Equality

James A. Buford Jr.

In the following viewpoint, James A. Buford Jr. asserts that minorities and women continue to be underrepresented in many types of jobs and concentrated in others, an indication that hiring decisions are not free from discriminatory practices. He contends that affirmative-action programs are effective in overcoming such discrimination. Requiring employers to use reasonable efforts to hire qualified minorities and women helps the economy by putting human resources to their most effective use and reducing expenditures for social services. Buford is a management consultant and a professor in the College of Business at Auburn University in Auburn, Alabama.

As you read, consider the following questions:
1. How does the author characterize the affirmative action debate?
2. Who makes most of the hiring decisions in the U.S. labor market and how does this work against minorities and women, in Buford's opinion?
3. According to the author, what affirmative-action safeguards prevent reverse discrimination against whites?

Reprinted, with permission, from "Affirmative Action Works," by James A. Buford Jr., *Commonweal*, June 19, 1998. Copyright © Commonweal Foundation.

You will, of course, wish to know my credentials for presenting a conservative case for affirmative action in employment. Well, first, as a social scientist with the requisite degrees and academic publications, I am licensed to diagnose the ills of the American workplace from my seat in the ivory tower. But I am also a management consultant with clients who often call on me to prepare their cases in fair-employment disputes, testify as an expert witness, and provide other services adversarial to plaintiffs claiming they have suffered discrimination. My politics are conservative and I have a strong Republican voting record. I live in Alabama, a state that takes a dim view of social engineering. I hold a professorship in the College of Business at Auburn University, not exactly a hotbed of liberal thinking. All this may give me an insider advantage in disputing the conventional wisdom of the Right, but my actual views on the issue at hand probably won't bring me an invitation to work on the civil rights platform plank at the next Republican convention.

Examining the Arguments

Apart from abortion, affirmative action is arguably the most loaded political issue of the day, and the least rationally argued. What passes for debate is mainly the clash of opposing evangelists with messages full of sound bites, catch phrases, and code words preaching disinformation to choirs of true believers. One choir gets the message: "Because you are black or female you are a victim and we are going to make them give you a job." The other choir hears: "They want to take away your job and give it to a black, or a female, or a black female." My effort will be to examine the facts and the arguments on the way to my conclusion, which is that affirmative action works rather well, at least in the context of employment. The points I will make apply less, if at all, to other race-conscious initiatives that carry this label.

Let's begin with the metaphor of the playing field. One argument is that the field was leveled in 1964 with the passage of Title VII of the Civil Rights Act. Or that, with more than thirty years of enforcement, it must be level by now. Well, it really is more level than it was. The mainly liberal view that equal employment opportunity somehow ended with the presidency of Ronald Reagan and that the Republicans spent twelve years turning back the clock is simply wrong. Republican presidents since Richard Nixon tended to be much more progressive on this issue than they were ever able to admit to their followers on the right. Most overt discrimination against blacks has ended. Systemic or unintentional discrimination resulting from seemingly neutral hiring practices, such as employment tests that commonly had an adverse effect on black applicants, were addressed by the 1971 Supreme Court decision in *Griggs v. Duke Power Company*.

Discrimination Is Real

Nevertheless, minorities and females continue to be underrepresented in many types of jobs and concentrated in others. For example, most of a company's accountants may be white and most of its custodians black. That may be because the company recruits for entry-level accounting jobs at colleges and universities where enrollment is predominantly white. Perhaps the company relies on employee referrals (the old-boy network). Another explanation has to do with how decisions are made when a pool of applicants includes both blacks and whites and it is necessary to select those who are "best qualified." A hiring decision is ultimately a judgment call made after a job interview by managers and supervisors with preconceived ideas about the attributes a candidate should have, attributes usually similar to their own. Although job interviews are a well-established management prerogative, research has shown that they are notoriously unreliable predictors of successful choices. Even at entry level, most individuals who make hiring decisions are white males; the higher the job level, the more this is likely to be the case. In the typical "multiple hurdle" hiring process, all the applicants who make it to the final pool are "qualified," and this group often includes minorities and women. Some do get hired, of course, and probably some are selected because they are black or female. In the aggregate, however, hiring officials tend to follow their instincts, and even in the absence of ill will or bias this works to the disadvantage of minorities and women. I have observed this pattern in my consulting practice, which, I should add, is not limited to the South. There are other factors that help to explain the under-representation of minorities and women in certain jobs, and sorting them out would be very difficult. But to say that discrimination is not part of the problem is about as credible as saying that it explains everything.

There are, of course, remedies for discrimination. An applicant who has been discriminated against can file a charge with the Equal Employment Opportunity Commission (EEOC).

The Bias at the Door

A job-hunting friend of mine, whom I'll call Lou, is sophisticated, polished and well-educated. Not long ago, he heard about a position in a small New Jersey town. It would take a long, two-hour drive to get there, but the hiring manager he spoke with on the phone was enthusiastic about his credentials. When he arrived, however, her enthusiasm vanished; so did the position. Something changed once she saw him. Lou, an African-American, was convinced the problem was his race.

Of course, we all carry weights—the societal resistance that must be overcome to achieve such life goals as a quality education and fulfilling employment. In this country, African-American ancestry has meant a difference in experience—a set of weights—of great endurance and heft. While members of other groups have certainly experienced discrimination, the immediately visible physiological differences of African-Americans sets them apart and leaves them more vulnerable to color-based snap judgments. The stereotypes commonly ascribed to blacks are more negative, plentiful and enduring than those ascribed to other groups. The remedy has required change not just on the part of the individual but on the part of the surrounding society as well.

Before you can open your mouth, hand over a resume or say "I graduated summa cum laude from Harvard," you immediately encounter and must overcome a going-in bias. Affirmative action has been an important remedy helping companies to push beyond that initial bias. Affirmative action's primary contribution may be the lens it has placed on the world that has made it suspicious when the qualified candidates for a particular opportunity overwhelmingly represent a single group.

Deborah Brown, "Why Affirmative Action Has Not Outlived Its Usefulness," www.fiveoclockclub.com/, 1996.

Even if the EEOC finds for the complainant, however, the agency cannot enforce its ruling but must take the case to federal court. Very few such cases are actually litigated by the EEOC; usually, the charging party is given a private right to sue. But the process is expensive and proving intentional discrimination is difficult. The employer need only state a "legitimate, nondiscriminatory reason" for the decision—for example, that a black applicant for an accountant position had less experience than a white applicant. Once the plaintiff would have been able to prevail—and to receive appropriate relief, including a job placement, back pay, and possible punitive and compensatory damages—by showing that the white applicant did not have more experience. But since the Supreme Court decision in *St. Mary's Honor Center v. Hicks* (1993), the plaintiff has been required to prove that the reason was a "pretext for discrimination"; he or she must uncover a prejudicial statement made by a hiring official, or a similar "smoking gun." That might have happened thirty years ago but today most employers are sophisticated enough to avoid doing or saying things that would expose them to legal risk.

"Reasonable Efforts," Not Quotas

But does this justify laws and regulations requiring employers to hire people because of their race or gender to meet quotas, thereby bringing about reverse discrimination—as was suggested in TV spots used by the Jesse Helms campaign in the 1996 Senate campaign in North Carolina? That does seem unfair, and apparently enough voters agreed to re-elect Senator Helms. Maybe such laws and regulations should be repealed outright, or, as [former] President Bill Clinton suggested, at least be fixed.

So let's look, beginning with Title VII of the Civil Rights Act as amended. The part on racial quotas is in 703(j), which says: "[No employer is required] to grant preferential treatment to any individual or group because of the race, color, religion, sex, or national origin of such individual or group on account of an imbalance that may exist. . . ." And legislation passed in 1991 discourages employers from using any such practices. No quotas here. So perhaps the problem rises not out of statutes but from regulations. Presidential Executive Order 11246, issued by Lyndon Johnson (LBJ) in 1965, established the Office of Federal Contract Compliance Programs, which requires employers with government contracts—a category that includes most major corporations as well as many small businesses, banks and other financial institutions, and colleges and universities—to have affirmative-action programs. That the order originated with LBJ definitely raises a flag for conservatives. But it was also signed by Richard Nixon, Gerald Ford, Ronald Reagan, and George Bush, who was so adamant about not having quotas one had only to read his lips.

Did these presidents fail to read what they were signing? Or did they actually read the order and decide it was reasonable? Perhaps they conferred with employer groups—overwhelmingly conservative and Republican—and learned that the business community was generally supportive. That, in fact, is how it happened. Furthermore, the order does not require preferential treatment or quotas. Rather, it requires covered employers to compare utilization of minorities and women in various job groups in their work force with the availability of qualified minorities and women in the relevant labor market. The key words here are "availability" and "qualified." That 35 percent of a given population is black does not mean that all of the blacks are qualified to be accountants. Availability would consider the percentage of blacks in the population but focus mainly on the component of that percentage qualified for a particular job. Where underutilization is found, employers are required to set goals and "use all reasonable efforts" to hire qualified minorities and women. Employers are allowed to establish these goals based on their own determination of availability.

Assume, for example, that a federal contractor has fifty accountants, of whom only two, or 4 percent, are black. The employer analyzes the relevant labor market and determines that the availability of qualified blacks is 10 percent. If ten accountants are to be hired this year, the employer would set a goal equal to availability, and attempt to hire one black applicant. In subsequent years, three more black accountants will be hired and underutilization will no longer exist in this job category with this employer. At this juncture, devotees of the level-playing-field metaphor might again make their point: that if affirmative action was ever necessary, it isn't necessary now. They're right—and that very same executive order anticipates their argument. Once the goal has been reached, the employer is no longer required—in fact, is not allowed—to set goals for hiring black accountants.

Some employers with no government contracts nevertheless adopt voluntary affirmative action plans. Underutilization of women and minorities exposes an employer to legal liability under the disparate impact theory of discrimination established by the *Griggs* decision. If a group of plaintiffs can identify hiring practices which appear to screen out blacks at a disproportionate rate, the burden is on the employer to justify those practices. In 1989, the Supreme Court decision in *Wards Cove Packing Co. v. Antonio* modified the case law, making it somewhat more difficult for plaintiffs to sue under the disparate impact theory, but Congress then enacted *Griggs* into the Civil Rights Act of 1991, signed by President Bush.

Safeguards Prevent Abuses

Doesn't this open the door to potential abuse? What about employers fearful of getting sued and therefore rushing to get their numbers up? There are probably some private employers who are sympathetic toward minorities and who want to be socially responsible. And, of course, the public sector is full of bleeding heart liberals. Won't both the supercautious and the hyperliberal go overboard in the direction of reverse discrimination?

No doubt some do, but such informal, ad hoc affirmative action is recognized and forbidden in case law. In *Daugherty v. Barry*, for example, a U.S. District Court ruled that the District of Columbia violated Title VII when eight eligible white applicants were bypassed in favor of two black applicants. The court found that the hiring decision was based on the city administrator's "personal vision" rather than a properly set goal. Not only case law but also federal regulations covering voluntary affirmative-action plans establish procedural safeguards—prohibiting, for example, laying off whites to maintain a racial balance or refusing to hire qualified white males—provisions very similar to those applying to government contractors.

Finally, in particular cases federal courts may require employers to adopt affirmative-action plans until they achieve compliance. In 1971 the Alabama Department of Public Safety had not been able to find even one black applicant qualified to be a state trooper, a problem that a federal judge solved by imposing an affirmative-action plan under which the judge determined availability, established goals, and instructed the department not merely to "use all reasonable efforts" but to "find and hire" qualified black applicants. Court-ordered plans imposed when discrimination is found to be pervasive and egregious can be much more stringent than voluntary plans or those required by executive order, but they are still designed to end when goals are met. Such cases are rare today, and most of the early orders have been vacated.

With the possible exception of this last category, it will be seen that affirmative action amounts to little more than a mildly proactive approach to equal employment opportunity. It most certainly does not impose gender and racial preferences or quotas, as its opponents would have us believe, nor does it go as far as its supporters would probably like. True, it is obviously not color-blind or gender-blind. Moreover, a basic tenet of conservative orthodoxy warns against being even mildly proactive; in the neoclassical school of economics (the one we attended), market forces are considered the appropriate means of dealing with social questions.

But the doctrine of market efficacy assumes free mobility of resources: Capital (equity or debt funding) flows to the enterprise where the return is highest, the latest technology is used, and human resources are deployed where their skills match the tasks to be performed. The underrepresentation of qualified minorities and women in certain jobs reveals a barrier to the mobility of human resources. Some neoclassicists would argue that an imperfect market is better than a governmentally regulated market; firms that do not hire the best-qualified workers of any race or sex will suffer, much as they would if they acquired too much debt load or chose the wrong accounting software. In the long run it all works out.

But, as [economist] John Maynard Keynes (admittedly not a neoclassicist) once pointed out, in the long run we are all dead. Moreover, discrimination in hiring imposes costs not only on individuals but on society; if human resources are not put to their highest and best use, the economy performs less well and expenditures for social services and income maintenance rise; and this violates another neoclassicist assumption, which holds that in a true market economy enterprises pay all the costs of production and do not shift them to society. To the extent that affirmative action matches up minorities and women with jobs for which they are qualified and are as likely as not to be "best qualified," the cost to the enterprise (and to the economy) becomes much smaller and in some cases disappears entirely. Perhaps conservatives should also ponder the possibility that that black accountant may find a better software package for the company's financial information system, receive a generous increase in salary, and become a Republican favoring more and better tax breaks for corporations.

More basically: As a conservative I recognize an obligation to support programs that promote personal responsibility and join opportunity with merit. That sounds a lot like what those people who conceived the "Contract with America" had in mind. If we expect people to buy into the work ethic, we might want to take steps to ensure that that attitude is rewarded. It is not good for an accountant always to be called and never to be chosen. It is not good for a welfare mother who has just completed a clerical-skills training program not to be able to find a job as a secretary. It is not good for the country when qualified women and minorities are underrepresented in many types of jobs.

Affirmative Action Works

Finally, again as a conservative I recognize an obligation to support programs that work as they are supposed to. And affirmative-action programs actually do work. That's especially true of those established by government contractors under the executive order. But many employers undertake this process on their own; in my consulting work I have observed the operation of such plans for a number of years, and the result has been a substantial increase in the numbers of both minorities and women in jobs that few or none could have obtained earlier. Of course there have been problems with affirmative action, but these tend to be the overdramatized exceptions that make it into TV spots. For the most part, affirmative action has escaped the unintended consequences that plague many social programs, and the progress has come without a great deal of bureaucratic complexity, without imposing unnecessary burdens of time and cost on employers, without creating barriers to employment of white males, and without creating ill will.

In the community of employment managers, testing professionals, attorneys, consultants, and academics who deal with affirmative action, I would expect to find some areas of disagreement with what I have argued, but most would agree that I have made a legitimate case. Why, then, do political leaders and commentators on both sides insist on making affirmative action into an issue like abortion, where the policy options represent fundamental philosophical differences and irreconcilable policy choices? Affirmative action is not a zero-sum game, and its merit does not depend on axioms of political correctness, liberal variety. Maybe we conservatives should actually embrace affirmative action as one of those rare government programs that further our agenda. How about a statement in "The Contract with America, Part II"?

"Affirmative action is an insidious policy that . . . is dishonest to the core."

Affirmative Action Does Not Promote Equality

Arch Puddington

Arch Puddington argues in the following viewpoint that affirmative-action programs reward incompetent minority businesses and individuals with employment opportunities in the interest of "diversity" and "expanding opportunity" for minorities, while passing over candidates with superior qualifications. This system of favoritism promotes mediocrity because it provides no incentive for less qualified minority job-seekers to improve their skills, according to Puddington. In the author's opinion, a private-sector initiative of programs that enhance black business skills and entrepreneurship would be preferable to government-mandated race preferences that lower standards and discourage hard work. Puddington is vice president of Freedom House, a non-profit organization working to advance economic and political freedom.

As you read, consider the following questions:
1. How does the experience of the author's friend "Michael" illustrate, in the author's opinion, the dishonesty behind affirmative-action programs?
2. Who are the "winners and losers" in the American workplace as a result of affirmative-action programs, according to Puddington?
3. In Puddington's opinion, why is the black civil-rights leadership resistant to restricting affirmative action to blacks?

Reprinted, with permission, from "Is Affirmative Action on the Way Out? Should It Be? A Symposium," by Arch Puddington, *Commentary*, March 1998. Reprinted with permission; all rights reserved.

A friend of mine has become acquainted with the real-life workings of the "diversity" idea. Michael works as a mid-level bureaucrat in the social-services department of a large Midwestern state. As part of his responsibilities, he reviews proposals submitted by care-providing agencies that do business with the state. He knows the strengths and weaknesses of each agency and agonizes before giving his opinion on the merits of a proposal. His integrity is legendary.

Recently, Michael has come under pressure to consider "diversity" in his calculations. Since there is no formal set-aside or affirmative-action policy for the contract-approval process, officials in his department have suggested various informal criteria—giving preference to agencies located in black or Hispanic neighborhoods, for example—in order to ensure that a specified percentage of contracts is awarded to minority-operated agencies. Michael is a confirmed Great Society liberal; he has, to my knowledge, never voted for a Republican. Nor is he dogmatic about the sanctity of the contract-awards process. He is not opposed to bending standards a bit to favor a promising minority agency. He will not, however, give assent to agencies with records of incompetence or whose proposals do not measure up.

But that is precisely what he is expected to do. Michael's superiors include a "diversity officer" whose job is to ensure minority hires and minority contracts. Whether an agency is effective at delivering services is of little concern to the diversity officer. Nor is racial discrimination; the agencies involved could not remotely be accused of bias, and their staffs include heavy proportions of blacks and Hispanics. But these facts do not detract from the diversity officer's mission. He dreams up schemes to implement de-facto set-asides; these schemes, it is understood by all, enjoy the support of higher-level officials and, especially, of elected state officials from minority districts.

Michael does not have final authority over the contracts. But because of his sound judgment and honesty, he commands the respect of his peers, and his opinions must be given serious weight. Meanwhile, officials of minority-run agencies have come to understand that a certain percentage of state grants has been, or should have been, reserved for them. They also regard Michael, a white male with high standards, as an adversary. They have called Michael a racist—behind his back, of course. In meetings, minority-agency officials justify claims to grants on the hackneyed grounds that only a black (or Hispanic or Asian) agency has the cultural sensitivity to serve the black (or Hispanic or Asian) community effectively.

There is no denouement to this story, just as there is no denouement to the affirmative-action controversy. Michael soldiers on, taking a firm stand in extreme cases, and making concessions in less outrageous instances. He remains a devoted liberal and retains a high sense of mission as a public servant. But personal experience has convinced him that affirmative action is an insidious policy that harms those who receive social services and makes him and other government officials complicit in a process that is dishonest to the core.

America's experience with affirmative action is rather neatly encapsulated in my friend's encounter with "diversity." In almost every instance, there are winners and losers. The winners are the undeserving agencies that win contract awards, and the diversity officials who take credit for "expanding opportunity" for minorities. The losers are the agencies that were passed over, despite their superior performance, and the social-service clients who are likely to receive subpar services. Some of the agencies passed over are large enough and wealthy enough to sustain the setback with no serious consequences; others, however, are small operations run by highly motivated and extraordinarily hard-working professionals. The loss of a major contract can mean a great deal to these smaller agencies.

If there is a social benefit in this particular case, it is that some minority agencies will take advantage of affirmative action to become effective in serving their community. Such cases do exist. Other agencies, having been rewarded despite a lack of qualifications, will see no reason to change. They will continue to rely on their friends in the government or the state legislature to press for a policy by which minority clients are served by minority agencies.

Here is the stuff of minor scandal. But the press will never touch the subject because everyone has a stake in remaining quiet, and because the press itself is compromised by its commitment to diversity in the newsroom. Affirmative action could never have survived if the press had devoted one-quarter of the coverage to the intricacies of its functioning that it devoted to the nuclear-power industry during the 1980's. Unfortunately, the integrity of the press is one more casualty of our misguided racial policies.

Politically Entrenched Supporters

As a means of "mending" affirmative action, some have suggested restricting it to blacks, as originally intended. This could actually serve as an important transitional step toward the eventual elimination of government-mandated race preferences. But one should not expect any serious action along these lines. The leadership of black civil-rights organizations may privately resent the inclusion of immigrant groups in a program designed to make amends for centuries of state-sponsored discrimination aimed at blacks. But they are unlikely to propose any scaling back of affirmative-action eligibility for fear of weakening what is emerging as a potent pro-preferences coalition.

This coalition, made up of blacks, Hispanics, and, to a lesser extent, Asian-Americans and liberal whites, represents a minority in national political affairs, but it is a larger group than many suppose. The rejection of an anti-preferences referendum in Houston in November 1997 demonstrates that affirmative action cannot be eliminated in cities where blacks and Hispanics constitute a majority, or even a near majority. In states with substantial minority populations, the chance of reducing affirmative action through the legislative process is increasingly remote.

If the elimination of affirmative action through normal political means is unlikely, we can nevertheless expect some erosion of its reach by the workings of economic competition and by the demands of Americans for higher standards in both the economy and government. The educational-standards movement is at heart a response to the pressures of the global economy, and it is worth noting that [former] President Clinton endorsed standards despite the opposition of minority politicians. Standards have also stiffened in certain industries as the production process becomes increasingly reliant on computers. Many police departments demand some college experience of new recruits.

Majority Rejects Race as "Deciding Factor"

Most Americans, black and white, dislike the truth behind racial preferences, and they make this dislike clear whenever the question is plainly put. A recent *New York Times*/CBS News poll found majorities of both races committed to the ends affirmative action is intended to achieve—overcoming the effects of discrimination, helping minorities to get ahead—but firmly opposed to the means now being used to reach them. The public likes the idea of aggressive recruitment and tutoring; it favors job training and mentoring and stringent laws to protect people from discrimination. But a clear majority (69 percent of whites and 63 percent of blacks) explicitly rejects the use of race as the deciding factor in a choice between two qualified candidates. An even more striking and unequivocal majority of two-thirds of blacks and 80 percent of whites dislikes the fact that less qualified people are being hired and promoted and admitted to college under the cover of affirmative action.

Tamar Jacoby, *Commentary*, March 1998.

This trend is likely to become more pronounced in the future, as is American impatience with the kind of duplicity and unfairness that my friend experienced and that is built into the diversity process. America does, however, face a very real problem in the continuing economic divide between blacks and everyone else in America. Given the fact that the outright elimination of preferential policies seems inconceivable over the short term, we should at least move toward a policy that uses affirmative action to deal with actual social problems. The foremost such problem is the failure of poor blacks to secure jobs in those parts of the economy where the opportunities of the future lie.

Turning to the Private Sector

The first step would be to jettison altogether the concept of diversity. Second, we should look to the private sector rather than government-enforcement agencies to develop a strategy for black advancement in the business world. There is ample precedent for this in business's voluntary involvement in education reform. Indeed, a private-sector initiative toward black economic advancement could be regarded as an adjunct to that involvement, starting with scholarships for business study or partnerships with community colleges or historically black colleges to develop programs that inculcate business skills and entrepreneurship.

The federal government could give this endeavor both moral and financial support. The United States already spends modest amounts to assist formerly Communist societies in their transition to a free-market economy. A similar but more ambitious initiative might be considered for America's inner cities. Unlike past urban-change ventures, however, government-funded initiatives would be implemented by private corporations rather than by government agencies.

As part of this strategy, private corporations would be given considerable latitude in establishing voluntary programs for hiring and promotion, with the understanding that the preeminent goal would be the integration of one group—blacks—into the private economy. In the meantime, the government would phase out over a few years those affirmative-action programs that entail government coercion.

There is, in fact, every reason to believe that business would be more effective at drawing blacks into the economic mainstream than is the case under the current affirmative-action regime. Under private-sector auspices, more attention would be paid to preparing young blacks for careers in the real economy. The corruption of the process by political intervention would be minimized. There would be an emphasis on meeting high standards rather than on reducing standards in order to meet a goal or quota.

I am under no illusions about the prospects for the replacement of affirmative action by a private-sector initiative. But America is a country full of surprises—witness the far-reaching changes in the welfare system enacted under a liberal Democratic President [Bill Clinton]. No policy that contradicts the very democratic premise of America can be expected to last forever, a fact that should be pondered by affirmative action's supporters before they gird themselves for all-out resistance to alternative arrangements.

*"Thirty-seven years after the Equal Pay
Act of 1963, American women working
full time still earn an average of 74 cents
for each dollar earned by men."*

Comparable Worth Policies Are Beneficial to Women

Naomi Barko

"Comparable worth" policies require employers to pay comparable wages to two people with comparable skills, education, and experience when they work at two different jobs. Naomi Barko asserts in the following viewpoint that such policies are effective in addressing the pay gap between men and women. In Barko's opinion, female-dominated occupations suffer from wage discrimination, leading women on average to earn only 74 cents for each dollar earned by a man. Comparable worth policies in Minnesota, Wisconsin, and Canada have proven successful at raising women's wages and have not adversely affected the labor market, according to the author. Barko is a journalist whose articles have appeared in the *New York Times, Ms. Magazine,* and other national publications.

As you read, consider the following questions:

1. What segment of the workforce is most adversely affected by the pay gap between men and women, in Barko's opinion?
2. According to the author, what arguments have long been given to explain women's lower pay?
3. How does the example of Milt Tedrow's job change illustrate the need for comparable worth policies, in the author's opinion?

H azel Dews is slightly embarrassed when you ask about her salary. She pauses and then confesses that after 25 years cleaning the Russell Senate Office Building in Washington, D.C. five nights a week, she makes barely $22,000 a year. That's not what really bothers her, though. What irks her is that men who do the same job earn $30,000.

Same Work, Less Pay

The men, she explains, are called "laborers." They can progress five grades. The women, however, are called "custodial workers," which means they can only advance two grades. "But," she protests, "they scrub with a mop and bucket. We scrub with a mop and bucket. They vacuum. We vacuum. They push a trash truck. We push a trash truck. The only thing they do that we don't is run a scrub machine. But that's on wheels, so we could do it too."

Thirty-seven years after the Equal Pay Act of 1963, American women working full time still earn an average of 74 cents for each dollar earned by men, according to a new report published jointly by the AFL-CIO and the Institute for Women's Policy Research (IWPR) in Washington. This affects all economic classes, but its impact is strongest on lower-income workers: If men and women were paid equally, more than 50 percent of low-income households across the country—dual-earner as well as single-mother— would rise above the poverty line.

New figures challenge the long-heard arguments that women's lower pay results from fewer years in the work force or time out for childbearing and rearing. The Women's Bureau of the Department of Labor cites a study by the president's Council of Economic Advisers showing that even in light of the vicissitudes of motherhood, 43 percent of the wage gap remains "unexplained," evidently due in large part to discrimination.

The Overview of Salary Surveys, published last year by the National Committee on Pay Equity (NCPE), summarized 23 surveys of specific salary titles conducted by professional associations and trade magazines. It reported that, for instance, among women engineers—where the salary gap averages 26 percent—women with the same qualifications continue to earn less than men even after they've been in the field for many years (20.4 percent less among women with a B.S. degree and 20–24 years of experience; 19.2 percent less among women with an M.S. and 20–24 years experience). Yet another study found that women physicians earned less than men in 44 of 45 specialties, including obstetrics-gynecology (14 percent less) and pediatrics (15.8 percent less), with lower compensation only partly explainable by hours worked or time spent in the field. And a 1999 report by the American Association of University Professors found that though women had grown from 23 to 34 percent of faculty since 1975, the salary gap had actually widened in that time period.

But the biggest reason for the pay gap is not discrimination against individual women but rather discrimination against women's occupations. As the percentage of women in an occupation rises, wages tend to fall. More than 55 percent of employed women work in traditional "women's jobs"—librarians, clerical workers, nurses, teachers, and child care workers. If these women are compared not to male workers, but to women with similar education and experience in more gender-balanced occupations, they would earn about 18 percent—or $3,446—less per year, according to the IWPR. (The 8.5 percent of men in these jobs earn an average of $6,259 less per year than men of comparable backgrounds working in "men's" fields.)

Why are "women's jobs" less lucrative? Is a truck driver—who earns an average annual wage of $25,030—really 45 percent more valuable than a child care worker who may have a four-year degree in early childhood education? Is a beginning engineer really worth between 30 and 70 percent more than a beginning teacher? Rarely, in the almost daily reports of teacher shortages, is it mentioned that the market alone cannot account for the striking disparity between teachers' and other professionals' salaries. No one ever suggests that it might have something to do with the fact that 75 percent of elementary and secondary schoolteachers are women.

In response to these disparities, women are beginning to mobilize. Three years ago, for example, Hazel Dews and 300 of her fellow women custodians joined the American Federation of State, County and Municipal Employees (AFSCME), which, after several futile attempts to negotiate, is now suing Dews's employer, the Architect of the Capitol, for equal pay. Since 1997, as women's membership in the labor movement has mushroomed to 40 percent, the American Federation of Labor–Congress of Industrial Organization (AFL-CIO) has conducted two surveys to discover the chief concerns of both union and nonunion working women. "And the runaway answer was equal pay," reports Karen Nussbaum, the director of the AFL-CIO's working women's department. Ninety-four percent of women in both surveys said equal pay was a top concern, and one-third—one-half of African-American women—said they did not have equal pay in their own jobs.

In 1999, calling pay equity a "family issue," the labor movement helped launch equal-pay bills in both houses of Congress and 27 state legislatures. Also in 1999, as Dews and her co-workers were demonstrating at the Capitol, the Eastman Kodak Company was agreeing to pay $13 million in present and retroactive wages to employees underpaid on the basis of either race or gender. The Massachusetts Institute of Technology, after protests by women faculty, made an unprecedented admission that it had discriminated against women "in salaries, space, awards, resources and response to outside offers."

Moreover, since 1997 the Office of Federal Contract Compliance Programs (OFCCP) has collected $10 million in equal-pay settlements from such corporations as Texaco, US Airways, Pepsi-Cola, the computer manufacturer Gateway, and health insurer Highmark, Inc. At the same time, two major national chains, the Home Depot and Publix Supermarkets, agreed to pay more than $80 million each to settle lawsuits based on sex discrimination.

Achieving Equality Through "Comparable Worth"

Recently, advocates have arrived at what they believe to be an effective means of generating pay equity—the concept of "comparable worth," which, as the name suggests, requires two people with comparable skills, education, and experience to be paid comparable amounts, even when they're working at two very different jobs. The Xerox Corporation, for example, uses comparable worth analysis, weighing such factors as education, experience, skill, responsibility, decision making, and discomfort or danger in working conditions, to set salary levels within the country. During the 1980s, some 20 state governments studied the comparable worth of their own employees and made adjustments totaling almost $750 million in increased pay to women. Minnesota, the leader in the field, has made pay equity adjustments in 1,544 counties and localities.

Perhaps the most dramatic argument for comparable worth, however, was made by a man. In the class action suit *AFSCME v. Washington State* in 1982, one of the nine named plaintiffs was Milt Tedrow, a licensed practical nurse (LPN) at Eastern State Hospital in Spokane. Approaching retirement and realizing that his "woman's" job wouldn't give him much of a pension, Tedrow switched to carpentry at the same hospital. To qualify as an LPN he had needed at least four years of experience, four quarters of schooling, and a license. As a carpenter, he was self-taught, had no paid work experience, and had no need of a license. And yet when he transferred from the top of the LPN wage scale to the bottom of the carpenter's, his salary jumped more than $200 a month—from $1,614 to $1,826. Why, Tedrow wondered at the time, does the state resent "paying people decently who are taking care of people's bodies, when they'd pay a lot for someone fixing cars or plumbing"?

Unions Fight Underpayment

Since then, the courts have ruled that evidence of unfair salaries is not enough to prove violation of the Equal Pay Act. Plaintiffs must prove that employers intentionally discriminated by lowering women's wages in comparison to men's. But some unions have prevailed on comparable worth questions by way of negotiations.

Service Employees International Union Local 715, for example, in Santa Clara County, just south of San Francisco, won nearly $30 million for 4,500 county employees, from secretaries to mental-health counselors. A study of some 150 job titles, performed by a consulting firm chosen jointly by the county and the union, showed that underpayment was common in job classes with more than 50 percent minorities, such as licensed vocational nurses and beginning social workers, and that 70 percent of such positions were filled by women. "We worked for at least three years to bring our male members along on this," says Kristy Sermersheim, Local 715's executive secretary. "When the county argued that in order to raise women's wages they'd have to lower men's, we refused to even discuss it. We kept regular pay negotiations completely separate."

Used by permission of Chris Britt and Copley News Service.

Another key to the local's success was the staunch support of allies among local women's groups. "We had 54 women's community groups on our side," reports Sermersheim. "The National Organization for Women, the American Association of University Women, the League of Women Voters, the Silicon Valley women engineers. . . ." On the day the county board of supervisors voted on whether to proceed with the study, the local delivered 1,000 pink balloons—symbolizing the pink-collar ghetto—to workplaces around the city. "We had balloons everywhere," recalls Sermersheim. "We had Unitarian women out there singing 'Union Maid.'"

It is this kind of coalition that pay equity advocates are counting on to push through the equal-pay bills now before state legislatures. Many of the new bills, unlike those passed in the 1980s, would extend comparable worth to private as well as public employees and would specifically extend benefits to minorities. Most are based on the fair pay act designed in consultation with the NCPE—a coalition of 30 women's, labor, civil rights, and religious groups—and introduced in Congress in 1999 by two Democrats, Senator Tom Harkin of Iowa and Representative Eleanor Holmes Norton of the District of Columbia. (A more modest paycheck fairness act, backed by the [former] Clinton administration, would toughen the Equal Pay Act of 1963 by removing present caps on damages and making it easier to bring class action suits.)

So far the new state bills have met with only modest success. The New Jersey and New Mexico legislatures have voted to study pay equity in both public and private employment, and Vermont's legislature voted to study just state employment. In Maine, where the new welfare laws gave rise to a commission to study poverty among working parents, it was discovered that the state already had a 1965 law on the books that mandated equal pay for both public and private employees and that specifically mentioned comparable worth. The state is now studying ways to put the law into effect.

Overcoming Resistance

Efforts like these have raised opposition from business and conservative groups. Economist Diana Furchtgott-Roth, a resident fellow at the American Enterprise Institute who recently represented business at an NCPE forum, supports "equal pay for equal work" but claims that comparable worth causes labor shortages because men refuse to take jobs where their wages will be tied to women's. "How can a government bureaucrat calculate if a secretary is worth the same as a truck driver, or a nurse as an oil-driller?"

In Ontario, Canada, Furchtgott-Roth says, where the practice of comparable worth is more common, day care centers are actually closing down because parents can't afford to pay for the higher salaries. But these charges turn out to be only partially true. Child care centers in Ontario were threatened when a Progressive Conservative government succeeded the liberal New Democrats and slashed funding. But the centers have not closed down. After a court challenge and an enormous public outcry, the provincial government is still subsidizing pay equity for child care workers (who, even with subsidies, earn an average of only $16,000 a year).

State employment officials in Minnesota and Wisconsin, two states with comparable worth laws, say that any labor shortages have far more to do with the tight labor market than with comparable worth. "There's a lot of flexibility in the law," says Faith Zwemke, Minnesota's pay equity coordinator. "For information technology people, for instance, we can give them signing bonuses and let them advance faster within the parameters of the policy."

Some male workers inevitably do resent women getting increases. "But many men can see pay equity as a family issue," says Karen Nussbaum of the AFL-CIO. A recent poll by Democratic pollster Celinda Lake showed that six out of 10 voters, both men and women, said equal pay was good for families.

Pay equity advocates had better be patient and persistent. The market has been biased against women at least since it was written in the Old Testament that when a vow offering is made to God, it should be based on the value of the person, and "[if] a male, from the age of twenty years up to the age of sixty years, your assessment shall be fifty silver shekels . . . and if it is a female, your assessment shall be thirty shekels." At this rate, winning equal pay may take a long time.

"No academic study says that equally qualified women make only 74 cents on a man's dollar."

Comparable Worth Policies Are Not Beneficial to Women

Diana Furchtgott-Roth

"Comparable worth" policies mandate that men and women performing different jobs be paid the same wages if the jobs require comparable skills and education. In the following viewpoint, Diana Furchtgott-Roth argues that these policies are unnecessary and have slowed job growth in several American states and Canada by raising business costs. According to the author, claims that women are forced into lower-paying occupations due to discrimination are false; equally-qualified women make about the same as men when occupation, age, and experience are taken into account. Furchtgott-Roth is a resident fellow at the American Enterprise Institute, a research organization dedicated to preserving and strengthening private enterprise.

As you read, consider the following questions:

1. Why does Furchtgott-Roth believe that the average wage gap between men and women of 74 cents on the dollar is "fiction"?
2. What arguments does the author make against receiving equal pay for performing the same job?
3. According to Furchtgott-Roth, how have comparable worth systems impacted Canadian taxpayers?

A recent article in *The American Prospect* by Naomi Barko repeats tired feminist claims that, due to discrimination, women earn only 74 cents on a man's dollar; that women are forced into lower-paying occupations; and that the only solution is government-mandated wage and salary controls, otherwise known as "comparable worth" or "pay equity" to make them seem more palatable.

Misrepresenting the Facts

The article is so riddled with errors that attempting corrections is like slapping at mosquitoes on a summer camping trip: It's impossible to hit them all. Closest to home, but least important, Ms. Barko claims that I represented business at a National Committee for Pay Equity forum in October 1999, in which I suggested that comparable worth would cause labor shortages. I am a resident fellow at the American Enterprise Institute, and I do not and have not represented any business organizations during my seven-year tenure.

Ms. Barko cites the "new" American Federation of Labor-Congress of Industrial Organizations (AFL-CIO) and the Institute for Women's Policy Research (IWPR) report. She is referring to the February 1999 report, "Equal Pay for Working Families: National and State Data on the Pay Gap and Its Costs." This report again propounded the fiction, repeated by Ms. Barko, that discrimination is responsible for the average wage gap between men and women of 74 cents on the dollar.

The 74 cents figure is derived by comparing the average median wage of all full-time working men and women. So older workers are compared to younger, social workers to parole officers, and, since full-time means any number of hours above 35 a week (and sometimes fewer), those working 60-hour weeks are compared with those working 35-hour weeks. To obtain figures for individual states, average wages of men and women within that state are compared in the same way. For example, in Louisiana, women's earnings are supposedly 67 percent of men's, whereas in the District of Columbia women earn 97 percent of men's wages.

But these estimates fail to consider key factors in determining wages, including education, age, part- or full-time status, experience, number of children, and, a related variable, consecutive years in the workforce. That is why in states such as Louisiana, where it is less common for women to work, and where they have less education and work experience, the wage gap is wider. In areas where it is more usual for women to work, such as the District of Columbia, the gap is smaller. But this average wage gap, as it is known, says nothing about whether individuals with the same qualifications who are in the same jobs are discriminated against.

Equal Qualifications—Equal Pay

The AFL-CIO/IWPR study calculated the cost of alleged "pay inequity" caused by the predominance of women and men in different occupational categories and concluded that "America's working families lose a staggering $200 billion annually to the wage gap," or, as Ms. Barko repeats, $3,446 per woman per year. But this number leaves out two major factors—the type of job, and the field of education. It is meaningless to say that the earnings of a man or a woman with a B.A. in English should be the same as the earnings of a man or a woman with a B.A. in math. So the study compares workers without regard to education or type of work: Secretaries are being compared with loggers, bookkeepers with oil drillers. Such numbers do not present an accurate estimate of wage gaps, and illustrate the difficulties of implementing the comparable worth proposals suggested by legislators.

How much less do equally-qualified women make? Surprisingly, given all the misused statistics to the contrary, they make about the same. Economists have long known that the adjusted wage gap between men and women—the difference in wages adjusted for occupation, age, experience, education, and time in the workforce—is far smaller than the average wage gap. Many economists, such as Columbia's Jane Waldfogel, Baruch College's June O'Neill, the University of Michigan's Charles Brown, and the New York Federal Reserve's Erica Groshen, find the difference to be only pennies on the dollar. I've said it elsewhere, but, at the risk of getting fired like Jeff Jacoby, I'll say it again: No academic study says that equally qualified women make only 74 cents on a man's dollar.

"Comparable Worth" Reduces Job Growth

Since average wage gaps occur naturally in labor markets for reasons described above, the only way to get rid of such gaps is to require not equal pay for equal work, but equal pay for different jobs. Comparable worth, as it is known, aims to end differences in pay across male- and female-dominated occupations by telling employers what they are allowed to pay workers in different occupations. Senator Daschle's Paycheck Fairness Act would have the Secretary of Labor draft "voluntary" wage guidelines for businesses—and voluntary guidelines sometimes have a way of becoming mandatory. Senator Harkin's Fair Pay Act would require all companies to have their own wage-guideline systems, enforced by the Equal Employment Opportunity Commission, to make sure that "equivalent jobs" of men and women were paid the same.

Explaining the Wage Gap

There are good reasons why the "average" woman earns less than the "average" man, almost all of which are connected to the fact that a woman's primary concern tends to be her family. The big difference between men and women is how they react to marriage and child-birth. Marriage tends to increase men's participation in the labor force and decrease women's. The hours men work tend to increase with the birth of a child. Hours that women work tend to decrease when a child is born. Mothers tend to work less overtime and take fewer jobs that will require that they work long hours in return for high pay than fathers do.

Marriage and child rearing contribute to a number of choices that women make that place them on a lower earning trajectory over time. Women have higher turnover rates and fewer continuous years on a single job than men do. More women work part-time jobs than men do, so they can devote time to the family. They also have a higher absence rate than men. Further, women tend to take those occupations where an absence of five to six years to raise a preschooler will not make them obsolete.

Shawn Ritenour, "Twenty-Four Cents," Ludwig von Mises Institute, 2001.

This is Soviet-style planning that caused Communist countries to rust and fade away while the West grew strong and prosperous. Ms. Barko describes the case of Milt Tedrow, a former nurse who decried the societal values that allowed him to earn more after switching to carpentry. It's probably worse that Britney Spears earns more than both of them put together, but that's how our society works. There is nothing to stop women from applying for carpentry jobs—or from trying to sing like Ms. Spears. But not all women who sing Ms. Spears's songs can be expected to earn her salary, because, even though the output may be equivalent, the amount that others are willing to pay is not.

Comparable-worth systems are wreaking havoc in Canada, which has had some forms of comparable worth since the Canadian Human Rights Act was passed in the mid 1970s. In 1999 courts ruled that the government has to pay billions in back pay to underpaid federal workers to settle "pay equity" suits. The 230,000 mostly female federal employees are due to receive $30,000 (Canadian) each, at a cost of about $3.6 billion, or $200 per Canadian taxpayer. Other Canadian employee groups are now preparing their own pay-equity suits.

It's well known that artificially raising wages lowers numbers of workers hired. Even Heidi Hartmann, director of the IWPR, testified at a Senate hearing that comparable worth has reduced job growth: "In Minnesota for example, employment grew by 4.8 percent but would have grown by 5.1 percent in the absence of pay equity implementation. Iowa and Washington, where pay adjustments were more expensive, did show some negative employment growth."

Millions of women try to enter the U.S. every year: Many die trying to do so, seeking the freedom to make their living in a land without economic restrictions such as comparable worth. In contrast, no one is dying trying to reach Communist Cuba. Our nation has the lowest unemployment rate and the highest growth rate of any industrialized country, and all women, whether working in paid jobs or working at home with children, benefit from a strong economy and job market. Let's keep it that way, rather than following other countries down the failed path of socialism.

> "The ADA [Americans with Disabilities Act] has positively affected workplace hiring and accommodation of people with disabilities."

The Americans with Disabilities Act Has Helped Disabled Workers

Brenda Paik Sunoo

The Americans with Disabilities Act (ADA) was passed in 1990 to address the disabled's high unemployment rate, which some attributed to employer discrimination and inaccessible workplaces. In compliance with the ADA, employers must make workplace modifications to accommodate the disabled. Brenda Paik Sunoo asserts in the following viewpoint that the ADA has accomplished its goal of improving employment opportunities and working conditions for the disabled. In the author's opinion, employers are reaching out to the disabled with more acceptance and are less inclined to consider a disabled employee a liability as a result of the ADA. Sunoo is a senior editor at *Workforce* magazine.

As you read, consider the following questions:
1. As reported by the author, what factors explain the disabled's improved employment rates?
2. What percentage of employers responding to a survey indicated that they have made their facilities more accessible to the disabled, according to Sunoo?
3. In addition to compliance with the ADA, what workplace improvements, according to the author, did Booz, Allen & Hamilton make to better accommodate the disabled?

From "Accommodating Workers with Disabilities," by Brenda Paik Sunoo, *Workforce*, February 2001; © 2001 all rights reserved. Reprinted with the permission of *Workforce*, Costa Mesa, California; www.workforce.com.

E d Ahern often thinks of himself as a mirror. As director of community development for eBility.com—a Santa Monica–based online community for the disabled—he's used to all kinds of facial reactions. "[People's] eyes get as far as my wheelchair and stop right there. They see me as a problem," he says. "The truth is, I've proven myself as an asset to any business."

Despite an orthopedic and neurological disability, Ahern works full-time at eBility.com. He has been employed there for five years. His role, he says, is to ensure that management and staff never lose sight of their Web site's audience. That means stimulating discussions on the site via message boards and chat rooms, recruiting community volunteers, and developing special events. In addition, he arranges for celebrities with disabilities to speak online.

In order to accommodate Ahern, eBility.com has provided him with a flexible work schedule. As long as he fulfills his job requirements, he can work between 7 A.M. and 2 P.M. "Days are easier for me," he says. The company also has provided him with an accessible work station. Although he can walk, he uses a wheelchair to ease the "lumbar-sacral plexus injury" that resulted from a car accident in 1991.

Tapping the Disabled Workforce

Indeed, 10 years after the Americans with Disabilities Act (ADA) of 1990, employees like Ahern have proven that having a disability doesn't mean one is a liability. At least, not any more than a non-disabled counterpart. Companies can, therefore, further tap this employable sector. Just look at the facts.

According to *American Demographics*, 15 million Americans have moderate to severe disabilities that don't interfere with their lives enough to keep them from working. That's good news for human resource (HR) recruiters. A disability, as defined by the ADA, applies to any individual who has a physical or mental impairment that substantially limits one or more major life activities, has a record of such an impairment, or is regarded as having such an impairment. Major life activities can include such things as caring for oneself, performing manual tasks, walking, seeing, hearing, speaking, breathing, learning, and working.

Considering the difficulties of filling today's job gaps, these additional figures are promising. They were cited by Patricia Rogan, president of the Association for Persons in Supported Employment (APSE) and associate professor at Indiana University School of Education:

• Fifty-six percent of people with disabilities who say they are able to work despite their disabilities are working today, compared to 46 percent in 1986.

• Two out of three unemployed people with disabilities would prefer to be working.

• Among 18- to 29-year-olds, 57 percent with disabilities are working, compared to 71 percent of their non-disabled counterparts, a gap of only 14 percent.

Improvements in employment rates, Rogan says, are most likely attributable to a variety of factors: improved school job training and transition services, the ADA, a strong economy, and developments in technology. In fact, according to Job Accommodation Network (JAN)—a service of the President's Committee on Employment of People with Disabilities—80 percent of job accommodations for the disabled cost less than $500.

So whether you're a small (under 500 employees), medium (500–5,000), or large (5,000 plus) company, is there really any major excuse for not hiring the disabled? There are still millions to choose from. If you have doubts, the three examples here may inspire new hiring possibilities.

A More Accepting Workplace

Individuals with mental disabilities often face the issues of public gossip and disclosure. Such was the case at American National Bank (ANB) in Cheyenne, Wyoming. In one situation, coworkers gossiped about a bank teller whom they described as "mentally incapacitated." The social isolation led to her eventual resignation, much to the dismay of her friend and coworker Deborah S. Mitchell.

Mitchell was hired as a mail clerk in February 1998. Her job description includes driving to ANB's various community banks to pick up their mail and bring it back to the main branch. She also puts stamps on envelopes and makes sure the mail gets to the post office on time.

Among her coworkers, Mitchell isn't perceived as being disabled. Indeed, she is one of the invisibly disabled, those who must cope with a mental impairment. Only HR manager Sandy Bordson and her supervisor are aware that the 37-year-old employee takes medication for paranoid schizophrenia and depression. "It controls my mood swings, fearfulness, and paranoia," she says.

ANB hired Mitchell after working in cooperation with a local mental health center. Its staff included a job coach who prepped her for the interview. Under the ADA, employers are not allowed to ask personal questions about disabilities. Nevertheless, Mitchell shared information about her impairment from the start, which enabled her employer to better accommodate her needs. For example, Mitchell experienced anxiety when she realized she would have to drive again after moving to Wyoming. Her job coach arranged for her to take driving lessons. She also was worried about safety on the road because of her night-vision problems. Mitchell's supervisor thus allowed her to finish the mail rounds by 5:30 or 6 P.M.

She also says that positive feedback goes a long way. It reduces her paranoia and stress about not fulfilling her work properly. Whenever her supervisor or coworkers pass by, a friendly word makes her feel welcome and at home. "I haven't had bad experiences here. They don't treat me like I have a disability," she says.

Although most coworkers don't know about Mitchell's impairment, HR is committed to educating its workforce about the disability community. By creating a culture of compassion and acceptance, companies can better tap workforce diversity. "We try to do at least two training sessions a year," says Bordson. Employees are provided information that explains how to work with employees—and customers— with disabilities.

Another way that ANB monitors its progress is through an assessibility survey, conducted by the city of Cheyenne. By participating in this poll, HR has learned new ways of providing better service. For example, the bank plans to place clipboards and deposit slips lower than usual, to better accommodate individuals in wheelchairs.

Bordson says that HR's biggest hurdle, however, is to overcome prejudice, and to make sure that HR looks at the skills and experience that applicants bring to the table.

The Price of Accommodation

Many employers worry that accommodating disabled individuals is expensive. But studies suggest that these costs are less than commonly assumed. Only about one in ten employers reports that costs of accommodating employees with disabilities have risen "a lot" as a result of the Americans with Disabilities Act, according to the 1995 Louis Harris/National Organization on Disability survey.

Between 1993 and 1995, Sears made a total of 71 documented accommodations, costing just $45 per accommodated worker, according to University of Iowa law professor Peter Blanck. Almost three-fourths (72 percent) cost nothing, he says. Seventeen percent cost less than $100, and 10 percent run between $100 and $499. In one case, $500 was spent to install restroom railings for an employee in a wheelchair.

Blanck says he did not factor in the cost of two relatively expensive accommodations, automatic doors and a system for entering computer data with verbal commands or Braille keyboards, because these could be used by all employees. In addition, he did not calculate indirect costs, such as those resulting from work schedule modifications or time spent on compliance-related duties. But Blanck says even with these costs factored in, it's still less expensive to accommodate than replace a qualified worker. At Sears, replacing an employee costs between $1,800 and $2,400.

Paula Mergenhagen, *American Demographics*, July 1997.

"Then, ask how we can accommodate the applicants. We want them to function as effective and happy employees."

Fortunately, the ADA has positively affected workplace hiring and accommodation of people with disabilities. A telephone survey titled "Implementation of the Employment Provisions of the ADA" asked 1,042 human resources managers (members of the Society for Human Resource Management) about ADA implementation.

The findings indicated that 82 percent have modified facilities to make them accessible; 79 percent have been flexible in applying human resource policies; 79 percent have restructured jobs or modified work hours; and 80 percent have changed the questions they ask during interviews and have made interview locations and restrooms accessible. In addition, 90 percent said their interview staffs were knowledgeable about asking questions related to job performance and abilities, rather than about disabilities.

Training and Support for Disabled Workers

Working among people with disabilities is like working a puzzle, says Leigh Ohlstein, human resources/risk manager at Portland Habilitation Center Inc. (PHC). "You fit the pieces together by learning what people need and can do."

PHC's mission is to train and employ individuals with disabilities. It is a multi-state, diversified, nonprofit organization that offers employees jobs in many fields. Among them are light manufacturing, administrative support, janitorial work, landscaping, emergency call operator, and mailroom clerk. "We are a union company," she says.

Out of approximately 700 employees, at least 75 percent are disabled. They range in age from 18 to 80 plus, says Ohlstein. "Our recruitment efforts are focused on that mission."

PHC began in the early 1950s, but its practices have evolved over the last 10 years. For example, the organization has focused on offering more varied jobs, benefits, and better wages to accommodate the different types of disabilities.

The growth created a need for more supervisors, thereby offering more opportunities for employees to move up into those roles. PHC also identified the needs of its employees and the barriers to keeping their jobs. So they improved employee benefits.

One of the needs identified was affordable housing. In 1998, PHC moved into the local housing arena and purchased low-income housing. "The [facilities] offered our employees and other qualified individuals affordable housing," Ohlstein says.

At the same time, the organization also created the position of retention coordinator within human resources. The position was established to be a resource to employees for matters that affect them on and off the job, such as performance and attendance issues. "Our goal is to hook up employees with outside community resources and internal resources, such as a supervisor or mentor," Ohlstein says.

Innovative Accommodations

PHC is then able to get both parties to problem-solve together. One innovative example involved a female janitor with a back injury and limited bending capacity. Her supervisor— also her husband—designed a "claw" with a magnet to pick up paper and paper clips and other items from the floor. The company also provided her with a lightweight vacuum cleaner and extended-handle duster. "All are simple and inexpensive measures to keep a person employed," says Ohlstein. In addition, the organization often seeks accommodation resources from injured-worker programs, the vocational rehabilitation program, and various social services agencies.

Workers with mental health and learning disabilities also are given consideration. Some have received extra, but limited, supervision. Instruction might include the use of checklists or visual aids or hands-on training. Moreover, those who've gone off their medications and develop poor-performance issues also are assisted with flexible policies. "We give those employees the opportunity to be off work for a period of time to stabilize and then return to work," she says. Sometimes this means a temporary separation from the company. The employee can return to work after his or her issue has been resolved.

Older workers (over 65) often pose a special HR challenge because their skill levels decline. As they lose their ability to perform the basic functions of their jobs, other workers have to pick up the slack, often creating a hardship. But as long as employees keep a team spirit, they can be paired accordingly. "We might team up a person who can't lift more than 15 pounds with someone who can," says Ohlstein. "The workload is evened out by having the latter do some of the former's tasks."

Getting others to help begins with creating a supportive work environment. That won't happen unless the individual with a disability is frank about his or her needs. Many times, it's not the accommodations that are the problem but how willing the individual is to assist in finding them, Ohlstein says.

Fortunately, the staff at PHC knows its employees and their struggles because of their open communication. "I know far more about our disabled employees than our non-disabled employees."

Ohlstein says she has watched hundreds of persons with disabilities blossom. When employers hire and accommodate the disabled, they also are supporting the economy and the community. "As disabled workers earn paychecks, they pay taxes and become consumers and stronger community advocates."

Finding Success with Disabled Employees

When you do right as a company, people hear about it. In 2000, *We* magazine—a lifestyle publication for persons with disabilities—named Booz, Allen & Hamilton one of the top 10 employers in the nation. *Business Week* also featured BAH's commendable track record in hiring the disabled. In addition, the company won the Employer of the Year Award from the Virginia Rehabilitation Services Association.

"It was an exciting year for us," says Meg O'Connell, an associate at Booz, Allen & Hamilton (BAH). She heads the commercial arm of the company's disability consulting team. She says the company's success rate is strongly driven by its community partnerships and internal programs. Virginia Rehabilitation Services Association, for example, has its own password to BAH's job postings online. Individuals with disabilities can thus access job opportunities from their homes. The management and technology consulting firm also is involved in a network of northern Virginia service providers of approximately 25 agencies.

Individuals with disabilities have been hired in all types of jobs, from mail clerk to partner, says O'Connell. Hiring workers with disabilities is no different from hiring any other diversity group. But ADA compliance is only the beginning. "We began making our facilities and our work environment user-friendly."

HR started with a task force made up of employees—on all levels—to identify areas of improvement. If you were to walk around the office today, you would see power-assisted doors on all major entrances and bathrooms, accessible seating in the auditorium, a company-wide accommodations fund, widespread use of interpreters at meetings, an assistive-technology demonstration area in the Systems Resource Center—among other accommodations.

In order to ensure such continual improvement, the task force recommended an employee forum. The Forum—as it is called—was established in 1999 and meets quarterly to discuss disability issues at work. Employees are able to offer suggestions, observe demonstrations of new assistive technology, and hear about new services.

"It's been such a big success," says O'Connell. "There are over 150 registered members of The Forum." More recently, BAH announced that The Forum had won the firm's internal Diversity Award for best forum of the year. (Booz, Allen & Hamilton sponsors several discussion groups for its diverse populations, such as African Americans, women, and gay and lesbian employees.)

Clearly, in all three examples—American National Bank, Portland Habilitation Center, and Booz, Allen & Hamilton—HR has been pivotal in boosting the hiring and retention of the disabled. According to Indiana University's Rogan, however, many obstacles to full employment still remain. Among the most prevalent are loss of benefits such as Medicaid, Supplemental Security Income [SSI], and SSDI [Social Security Disability Insurance], transportation, skills training, personal assistance, and negative public attitudes.

Given the fact that 2000 was the 25th anniversary of the Individuals with Disabilities Education Act (IDEA), consider renewing your employer commitment to the following:

• Full implementation of and compliance with the ADA and IDEA

• Increased outreach and technical assistance so that people with disabilities and families are educated on their rights under the ADA and IDEA

• Adequate funding for monitoring, oversight, and enforcement of ADA and IDEA

If you have a job opening coming up, take the "dis" out of disability—and watch your company grow.

> "*The employment provisions of the
> Americans with Disabilities Act (ADA)* . . .
> *have* harmed *the intended beneficiaries
> . . . not helped them.*"

The Americans with Disabilities Act Has Not Helped Disabled Workers

Thomas DeLeire

In the following viewpoint, Thomas DeLeire contends that the Americans with Disabilities Act (ADA), enacted in 1990 to increase job opportunities for people with disabilities, has unintentionally led to less employment of disabled workers. According to DeLeire, under the "reasonable accommodation" provision of the ADA, employers may be required to make costly modifications to the workplace and are increasingly faced with lawsuits when disabled employees feel that their accommodation needs have not been met. Fearing these negative consequences, employers have reduced their hiring of the disabled, in the author's opinion. DeLeire is an assistant professor at the Harris Graduate School of Public Policy Studies at the University of Chicago.

As you read, consider the following questions:

1. According to DeLeire, what percentage of men and women in the working-age population reported a health impairment that limited their capacity to work?
2. In the author's opinion, which segments of the disabled population are most affected by ADA's reduction in employment opportunities?

Excerpted from "The Unintended Consequences of the Americans with Disabilities Act," by Thomas DeLeire, *Regulation*, vol. 23. no.1 (2001). Reprinted with permission from the Cato Institute.

E conomists commonly lament public policies that transfer resources to a particular group because such policies ignore the "law of unintended consequences." Economists point out, for example, that the law of unintended consequences is at work when workers' wages fall in response to a mandated increase in benefits or when employment falls in response to an increase in the minimum wage. As Henry Hazlitt said in *Economics in One Lesson*, "Depth in economics consists in looking for all the consequences of a policy instead of merely resting one's gaze on those immediately visible."

Higher Costs, Less Hiring

The employment provisions of the Americans with Disabilities Act (ADA) exemplify the law of unintended consequences because those provisions have *harmed* the intended beneficiaries of the Act, not helped them. ADA was enacted to remove barriers to employment of people with disabilities by banning discrimination and requiring employers to accommodate disabilities (e.g., by providing a magnified computer screen for a vision-impaired person). However, studies of the consequences of the employment provisions of ADA show that the Act has led to less employment of disabled workers.

Why has ADA harmed its intended beneficiaries? The added cost of employing disabled workers to comply with the accommodation mandate of ADA has made those workers relatively unattractive to firms. Moreover, the threats of prosecution by the Equal Employment Opportunity Commission (EEOC) and litigation by disabled workers, both of which were to have deterred firms from shedding their disabled workforce, have in fact led firms to avoid hiring some disabled workers in the first place.

That result is not surprising to students of economics. After all, if you raise the price of a good or service, you must expect that less of it will be bought. Likewise, theories of labor demand predict that when a group of workers becomes more expensive, firms will hire other workers or substitute capital for labor.

Disabled Americans are a large and economically disadvantaged group. In 1995, according to the Survey of Income and Program Participation (a nationally representative survey that queries individuals about their disability and employment status), 11.6 percent of men and women in the working-age population (ages 18 to 65) reported a health impairment that limited either the type or amount of work they could do. That percentage has been rising: in 1986, for example, 9.6 percent of the working-age population reported a disability.

We commonly think of the intended beneficiaries of ADA as persons with mobility, vision, or hearing impairments. ADA, however, covers a vast number of health impairments. The Act defines a disability as "a physical or mental impairment that substantially limits one or more major life activities, a record of such an impairment, [or] being regarded as having such an impairment." Major life activities include walking, lifting, seeing, hearing, breathing, and—most importantly for the employment provisions of ADA—working. In fact, mobility, vision, and hearing impairments represent merely 17 percent of the population of men with disabilities. By far the most prevalent of disabilities reported in surveys are bad backs and heart disease. Thus, ADA covers many more people than those commonly thought of as disabled. On the other hand, the disabled who are most often portrayed in newspaper articles about the excesses of ADA—the mentally disabled and substance abusers—represent only 6.7 percent of the disabled population.

As a group, people with disabilities earn less than people without disabilities. Despite receiving government-provided benefits, people with disabilities have relatively low incomes. The average annual income (including government transfers) of disabled men was only 61 percent of that of nondisabled men in 1992, and labor earnings of disabled men averaged only 47 percent of the earnings of nondisabled men.

These differences in earnings are explained partly by the fact that fewer people with disabilities work: only 53 percent of disabled men work compared with 89 percent of nondisabled men. However, disabled workers also receive lower pay when they do work; their average wage is only 79 percent of the average wage of nondisabled workers. In addition, people with disabilities often are additionally disadvantaged in that they are generally less educated, older, and employed in less-skilled occupations than are the nondisabled.

The fact that disabled people work less and earn less when they work is consistent with the view that people with disabilities face barriers in the labor market. The same fact is also consistent with the (almost tautological) view that a disability reduces a person's productivity.

How ADA Works

The employment mandates of ADA have two broad goals. One goal, which is similar to that of other civil rights legislation, is to ensure that people with disabilities have access to types of employment from which they traditionally have been excluded. The second goal, which is similar to that of antipoverty programs, is to increase job opportunities for disabled people. Therefore, the employment provisions of ADA consist of two parts:

> • Section 101(8) prohibits wage and employment discrimination against "qualified individuals with a disability." A qualified individual with a disability is "an individual with a disability who, with or without reasonable accommodation, can perform the essential functions of the employment position."

> • Section 101(9) requires an employer to provide a "reasonable accommodation"—a change in the work environment that results in an equal employment opportunity for a person with a disability.

To meet the reasonable accommodation provision of Section 101(9), an employer may be required to modify facilities, redefine jobs, revise work schedules, provide special equipment or assistance, give training or other forms of support, or eliminate nonessential job functions. A business can avoid an accommodation only if it would cause "undue hardship" to the nature or operation of the business.

The mandates of the ADA have a major effect on employment decisions because of the costs they can impose. Section 101(9) is a significant element of ADA's employment provisions because providing reasonable accommodations can be costly for employers. Unfortunately, there is little evidence about the costs of accommodation. The evidence at hand comes from the President's Job Accommodation Network (JAN) and studies of federal contractors under the Rehabilitation Act of 1974, such as the study conducted by Berkeley Planning Associates (BPA) in 1982. JAN reports that the median accommodation under ADA costs $500 or less. The BPA study found that the average cost of an accommodation is very low—approximately $900—and that 51 percent of accommodations cost nothing.

Table 1. Effect of ADA on Employment of Men with Disabilities

	Employment rate (percent) and change in employment rate (percentage points)	
	Men with disabilities	Men without disabilities
Before enactment of ADA (1985–1990)	59.8	95.5
After enactment of ADA (1991–April 1995)	48.9	92.4
Change in employment rate	−10.9	−3.1
Employment effect of ADA	−7.8	

In spite of such results, it would be wrong to conclude that ADA has little effect on employers. First, both sources underestimate the costs of accommodation by including only monetary costs. Allowing a disabled employee to work a more flexible schedule, for example, might not increase a firm's out-of-pocket expenses, but it does increase a firm's costs.

Second, the burden of ADA is not the less-expensive accommodations that very likely would have been made even in the absence of a government mandate but rather the more expensive ones. According to JAN, 12 percent of accommodations cost more than $2,000 and 4 percent cost more than $5,000. The BPA study found that 8 percent of accommodations cost more than $2,000, 4 percent of accommodations cost more than $5,000, and 2 percent of accommodations cost more than $20,000.

The costs of litigation resulting from ADA also can be high. Since enforcement of the Act began in July 1992, it quickly has become a major component of employment law—one to which employers increasingly have had to respond. Through the end of fiscal year 1998, 108,939 ADA charges had been filed with EEOC, and 106,988 of those charges had been resolved. Of the resolved charges, 86 percent were either dropped or investigated and dismissed by EEOC but not without imposing opportunity costs and legal fees on employers. The other 14 percent of the charges led to a finding of discrimination by EEOC or a private settlement at an average cost to employers of $14,325 (not including opportunity costs and legal fees).

Although employers can be and are sued for discriminatory hiring, most litigation under ADA arises when employees are fired. The two most common violations of ADA alleged in charges filed with EEOC have involved, first, discharge, layoff, or suspension and, second, failure to provide reasonable accommodation. Thus, firms may have responded to the prospect of litigation by reducing their hiring of the disabled.

Has ADA Worked as Intended?

Although ADA may have caused employers to accommodate people with disabilities, the cost of complying with the Act may have reduced the demand for disabled workers and thereby have undone ADA's intended effects. To determine the employment effect of ADA, I analyzed data for a sample of men aged 18 to 65 from the Survey of Income and Program Participation (SIPP).

Table 1 compares changes in the employment rates of disabled and nondisabled men before and after enactment of ADA. Employment of men with disabilities fell by 10.9 percentage points following the enactment of ADA, while employment of nondisabled men fell by 3.1 percentage points. Thus, ADA reduced the employment of disabled men by 7.8 percentage points.

Has ADA reduced employment of disabled workers of all types or have ADA's negative effects been concentrated in a few demographic categories? Using the sample of working-age men from the SIPP data, I estimated the effects of ADA on employment rates for disabled men according to their level of education, type of disability, and age (specified by decade of birth). I controlled for such other factors as occupation, industry, minority status, length of disability, and whether a disability resulted from an injury. . . .

To summarize:

• ADA caused a decrease of about 8 percentage points in the employment rate of men with disabilities.

• ADA caused lower employment regardless of age, educational level, and type of disability.

• Those most affected by ADA were young, less-educated and mentally disabled men.

ADA is a striking example of the law of unintended consequences. ADA has reduced employment opportunities not only for disabled people as a whole but especially for the most vulnerable groups—the young (less experienced), less educated (less skilled), and mentally disabled—groups that find it most difficult to get jobs.

Why has ADA had these consequences? Firms generally have reduced their employment of the disabled because the Act has imposed higher accommodation costs than firms would voluntarily incur. The burden of cost has fallen especially hard on those workers least likely to have been accommodated voluntarily by firms in the absence of ADA, namely, less-experienced and less-skilled workers and workers with mental disabilities, which generally are more difficult to accommodate than physical disabilities. . . .

What Should We Do?

Substantial barriers to the employment of people with disabilities persist in spite of the employment mandates of ADA. In fact, the threat of litigation and ADA's accommodation mandate may even raise the barrier for many disabled workers by raising the cost of hiring them.

What policies would better assist the disabled? If the cost of the accommodation mandate has led employers to reduce their employment of the disabled, should the nondiscrimination mandate be enforced more rigorously so as to raise the cost of noncompliance? Or is there a need for a new strategy for increasing the employment of disabled Americans?

One new strategy that holds promise is to create a Disabled Workers Tax Credit (DWTC)—modeled on the Earned Income Tax Credit (EITC)—as proposed by Richard Burkhauser, Andrew Glenn, and D.C. Wittenburg. DWTC would provide a wage subsidy for disabled workers to encourage them to remain in or reenter the workplace after becoming disabled. The wage subsidy, even if given directly to workers, effectively would reduce the cost of hiring and accommodating them. That, in turn, would increase the ability of firms to hire them.

Although DWTC is still being assessed, experience with EITC suggests that DWTC could work. Empirical studies have found EITC to be successful at increasing labor force participation and reducing poverty among poor families. . . .

Although a DWTC-like program would be yet another government program, it is likely to be both cheaper and more effective than forcing the hiring of disabled workers through the employment mandates of ADA.

Periodical Bibliography

The following articles have been selected to supplement the diverse views presented in this chapter. Addresses are provided for periodicals not indexed in the *Readers' Guide to Periodical Literature*, the *Alternative Press Index*, the *Social Sciences Index*, or the *Index to Legal Periodicals and Books*.

Natalie Angier — "Exploring the Gender Gap and the Absence of Equality," *New York Times*, August 25, 1998.

Michael Bernick and Catherine Campisi — "Removing Disabilities As Job Barriers," *San Diego Union-Tribune*, January 3, 2001.

Tim Bonfield — "Americans with Disabilities Act Law 10 Years Old," *Cincinnati Enquirer*, July 26, 2000.

Robert Cherry — "Black Men Still Jobless," *Dollars & Sense*, November/December 1998.

Christian Science Monitor — "Gains for Working Women," January 8, 1998.

Robyn D. Clarke — "Has the Glass Ceiling Really Been Shattered?" *Black Enterprise*, February 2000.

Commentary — "Is Affirmative Action on the Way Out? Should It Be? A Symposium," March 1998. Website: www.commentarymagazine.com/9803/symp.html.

W. Michael Cox and Richard Alm — "Death by Living Wage," IntellectualCapital.com, June 29, 2000. Website: www.intellectualcapital.com.

Christina Duff — "Why a Welfare 'Success Story' May Go Back on the Dole," *Wall Street Journal*, June 15, 1999.

The Economist — "The Widening Gap: Does Technology Hurt the Poor?" February 3, 2001.

Jonathan Barry Forman — "Why Treat Today's Women As If This Were the 1930s?" *Los Angeles Times*, May 4, 1997.

Diana Furchtgott-Roth — "Comparable Worth in Theory and Practice," Lexington Institute, November 1999. Website: www.lexingtoninstitute.org/whatworks/whtwrks12.htm.

Ellen Goodman — "The Issue of Pay Equity Is Back," *Boston Globe*, March 22, 1999.

Paul Kivel — "Affirmative Action Works!" *In Motion Magazine*, n.d. Website: www.inmotionmagazine.com/pkivel.html.

Robert Kuttner   "Making Sure Workers Live Decently," *San Diego Union-Tribune*, August 17, 1997.

Glenn C. Loury   "Tenuous Trickle-Down," *New York Times*, May 29, 1999.

Debra E. Meyerson   "A Modest Manifesto for Shattering the Glass
and Joyce K. Fletcher   Ceiling," *Harvard Business Review*, January 2000.

David Moberg   "Martha Jernegons's New Shoes," *American Prospect*, June 19–July 3, 2000.

Walter Olson   "In the Land of the ADA, the One-Eyed Man Is King," *Wall Street Journal*, June 22, 1998.

Robert Reich   "The Great Divide," *American Prospect*, May 8, 2000.

Robert E. Rubin et al.   "What's a Minimum Wage Job Worth?" *Wall Street Journal*, April 1, 1996.

Charlene Marmer   "Women Are Still Undervalued: Bridge the
Solomon   Parity Gap," *Workforce*, May 1998.

Victoria Stanhope   "Working Women: Short of Time and Money," *Off Our Backs*, December 1997.

J.D. Tuccille   "Living with Living Wage Laws," Free-Market.net, October 25, 2000. Website: www.free-market.net/spotlight/livwage/.

Wall Street Journal   "Repeal the Minimum Wage," April 29, 1996.

For Further Discussion

Chapter 1

1. Anthony P. Carnevale contends that job training programs will help reduce unemployment, underemployment, and income disparity. Anita Hattiangadi argues that taxpayers already spend over $20 billion dollars on job training programs every year with unimpressive results. Do you believe that taxpayer dollars should be used to ensure the success of those with limited skills in the job market? Why or why not?

2. Robert W. Schaffer believes that school-to-work programs represent a dangerous shift in the public education system away from academic preparation toward training children for often unchallenging jobs. After reading this viewpoint, do you think a greater emphasis should be placed on academics or preparing students to find a job after graduation? Why? Have you had any work experiences that have made getting an education seem more worthwhile to you? Explain your answer.

3. Steve Kangas asserts that it is wrong to expect elementary and high school teachers to teach specialized skills and that apprenticeship programs would better prepare those not attending college for jobs in the high-tech economy. Do you believe that learning highly specialized skills will improve or limit a person's chances in the job market? Would it be more effective for high school graduates to improve their basic math, writing, and computer skills, as advocated by Richard J. Murnane and Frank Levy? Explain your answer.

Chapter 2

1. David Boaz is a proponent of the economic theory of libertarianism, which advocates minimizing government regulations on businesses so that they can conduct their activities with less restrictions and lower taxes. Boaz claims that government intervention in the free market cannot solve the problem of unemployment and will hurt the overall economy. Do you agree with his opinion, or can government create jobs for the unemployed without impairing the economy, as Dimitri B. Papadimitriou contends? Support your answer with references to the viewpoints.

2. Ron Haskins asserts that welfare-to-work programs are successful because of their emphasis on "work first" before job training or further education. Randy Albelda asserts that pushing poor mothers into dead-end jobs without training is only perpetuating

a cycle of poverty. Which author makes the more convincing argument? Is it fair to expect able-bodied people on public assistance to support themselves through work, even though they may lack the skills for a middle-income job? Why or why not?

3. Jill Jenkins argues that "living wage" laws mandating higher wages for entry-level workers who possess few job skills will force affected businesses to reduce hiring or relocate to less expensive locations. While the workers who remain employed will most likely benefit from increased wages, are laws that risk making it harder for low-skilled job candidates to find work a meaningful approach to helping low-wage earners? Is a minimum-wage job better than no job at all? Explain.

Chapter 3

1. After reading the viewpoints by Amy B. Dean and Kevin Hassett, do you believe that labor unions will become more or less attractive to U.S. workers looking for a stable workplace? Explain you answer.

2. Reed Larson argues that it is not fair for workers in states without right-to-work laws to be compelled to contribute dues to unions they may not wish to join. William L. Clay contends that in requesting a contribution from all workers, unions are operating in a fair and democratic manner. Whose position makes the most sense, given democratic principles of "majority rules"? Is it fair for workers in right-to-work states to withhold dues and act as "free riders"? Why or why not?

3. John J. Sweeney asserts that contingent workers deserve the protection that labor unions can provide in increased bargaining leverage with employers and better health and pension benefits. How will contingent workers, employed in many different occupations under varying conditions of employment, find a common basis around which to unionize? Do you think that contingent workers, many of whom prefer the flexibility of temporary and contract work, will find a less favorable, more rigid job market if they join unions in large numbers? Explain.

Chapter 4

1. Naomi Barko uses the example of Milt Tedrow, a former nurse who earned more money after becoming a carpenter, to illustrate her contention that women working in female-dominated occupations are paid less than men with comparable skills and education. What argument does Diana Furchtgott-Roth make against this illustration? Whose use of this example is more ef-

fective? Do you believe that a nurse should be paid the same as a carpenter? Explain your answer.

2. James A. Buford Jr. argues that laws are justified in requiring employers to make reasonable efforts to hire women and minorities, and he specifically points out that safeguards are in place to prevent the abuse of affirmative action. He also asserts that without affirmative action, more qualified minorities and women would be passed over for jobs in favor of white males. Arch Puddington believes that many of the beneficiaries of affirmative action are unqualified for the positions they fill. Which argument is the most compelling? Should less qualified minorities and women be given jobs for the sake of diversity, or is this unfair to more competitive job candidates? Explain your answer.

3. Thomas DeLeire describes how businesses are required to modify workplace facilities, revise work schedules, and redefine jobs to accommodate disabled employees under the Americans with Disabilities Act (ADA). What do you think are some of the problems confronting both employers and the disabled in creating a more accommodating workplace? Does compliance with the ADA place an unfair burden on the employer? Explain.

Organizations to Contact

The editors have compiled the following list of organizations concerned with the issues debated in this book. The descriptions are derived from materials provided by the organizations. All have publications or information available for interested readers. The list was compiled on the date of publication of the present volume; the information provided here may change. Be aware that many organizations take several weeks or longer to respond to inquiries, so allow as much time as possible.

American Association for Affirmative Action (AAAA)
1600 Duke St., Suite 700, Alexandria, VA 22314
(800) 252-8952 or (703) 299-9285 • fax (703) 299-8822
e-mail: execdir@affirmativeaction.org
website: www.affirmativeaction.org

AAAA is a group of equal opportunity/affirmative-action officers concerned with the implementation of affirmative action in employment and education nationwide. Its publications include the quarterly *AAAA News.*

American Federation of Labor-Congress of Industrial Organizations (AFL-CIO)
815 16th St. NW, Washington, DC 20006
(202) 637-5000 • fax: (202) 637-5058
e-mail: feedback@aflcio.org • website: www.aflcio.org

The AFL-CIO is a voluntary federation of sixty-four national and international labor unions representing 13 million working men and women. It leads the labor movement in its efforts to organize workers through recruitment, education, training, and political activities. The AFL-CIO's publications include the biweekly newsletter *AFL-CIO News.*

American Institute for Full Employment
2636 Biehn St., Klamath Falls, OR 97601
(541) 273-6731 • fax: (541) 273-6496
website: www.fullemployment.org

The institute is a nonprofit organization that conducts research to develop the best means of achieving employment for all Americans able to work. It believes that full employment can be attained by unleashing the free market and minimizing or eliminating government intervention. The institute publishes the quarterly newsletter *S.T.E.P.S.* along with reports on getting people off welfare and into meaningful jobs.

Association for Union Democracy (AUD)
500 State St., Brooklyn, NY 11217
(718) 855-6650 • fax: (718) 855-6799
e-mail: aud@igc.org • website: www.uniondemocracy.org

AUD is a pro-labor, nonprofit organization that advocates a stronger democratic voice for union members within unions and works to ensure members' legal rights. It provides organizing, educational, and legal assistance to union members and publishes the bimonthly *Union Democracy Review* and numerous books on labor issues.

The Brookings Institution
1775 Massachusetts Ave. NW, Washington, DC 20036-2188
(202) 797-6104 • fax (202) 797-6319
e-mail: brookinfo@brook.edu • website: www.brook.edu

The institution is a private, nonprofit organization that conducts research on economics, education, foreign and domestic government policy, and the social sciences. Its principal purpose is to contribute informed perspectives on the current and emerging public policy issues facing the American people. Its publishes the quarterly *Brookings Review* and many books through its publishing division, the Brookings Institution Press.

The Conference Board
845 Third Ave., New York, NY 10022-6679
(212) 759-0900 • fax: (212) 980-7014
website: www.conference-board.org

The Conference Board is a worldwide business membership and research network linking executives from different companies, industries, and countries with economic data, forecasts, and business analysis. Its purpose is to enhance the contribution of business to society by conducting research on a wide range of business problems. It publishes research reports on topics such as workforce diversity and companies' community involvement, along with the bimonthly magazine *Across the Board*.

Economic Affairs Bureau
740 Cambridge St., Cambridge, MA 02141-1401
(617) 876-2434 • fax (617) 876-0008
e-mail: dollars@dollarsandsense.org
website: www.dollarsandsense.org

The bureau publishes and distributes educational materials that interpret current economic information from a progressive, socialist perspective. It publishes the monthly magazine *Dollars & Sense*.

Economic Policy Institute (EPI)
1660 L St. NW, Suite 1200, Washington, DC 20036
(202) 775-8810 • fax (202) 775-0819
e-mail: epi@epinet.org • website: www.epinet.org
EPI conducts research and promotes education programs on economic policy issues, particularly the economics of poverty, unemployment, and American industry. It supports organized labor and believes that government should invest in infrastructure to improve America's economy. It publishes the quarterly *EPI Journal* and the monthly *EPI News*, which details its latest research publications.

Employment Policies Institute (EPI)
1775 Pennsylvania Ave. NW, Suite 1200
Washington, DC 20006-4605
(202) 463-7650 • fax (202) 463-7107
e-mail: epi@epionline.org • website: www.epionline.org
The institute is a nonprofit research organization that believes entry-level employment opportunities often provide the best job-training opportunities for young Americans and those seeking to move from welfare to work. It also believes that a government-set minimum wage destroys these opportunities. EPI publishes numerous articles on low-wage workers and the negative effects of raising the minimum wage.

Employment Policy Foundation (EPF)
1015 15th St. NW, Suite 1200, Washington, DC 20005
(202) 789-8685 • fax: (202) 789-8684
e-mail: info@epf.org • website: www.epf.org
EPF provides nonpartisan research on federal, state, and local employment policy to policy makers and the public. Its areas of research include workplace, workforce, and employment trends; training and education; pay equity; unions and collective bargaining; minimum wage and living wage; and temporary work. EPF publishes numerous books on these topics, including *Workplace Policy for the New Economy*.

Families and Work Institute
330 Seventh Ave., 14th Floor, New York, NY 10001
(212) 465-2044 • fax (212) 465-8637
e-mail: mlambert@familiesandwork.org
website: www.familiesandwork.org
The institute is a nonprofit research and planning organization dedicated to developing new approaches to balancing workplace productivity with the changing needs of the American family. Nu-

merous publications are for sale on the institute's website, including *Faces of the Low-Wage Workforce* and *The Changing Workforce: Highlights of the National Study.*

Family Research Council
801 G St. NW, Washington, DC 20001
(202) 393-2100
website: www.frc.org

The council provides information to the public on issues such as parental responsibility, the impact of working parents on children, the effects on families of the tax system, and community support for single parents. Its publications include the *Ideas and Energy* webzine, the monthly *Washington Watch*, the bimonthly *Family Policy*, and the *Insight* papers published two to three times per month.

Independent Women's Forum (IWF)
PO Box 3058, Arlington, VA 22203-0058
(800) 224-6000
website: www.iwf.org

IWF is an organization that advocates less government regulation of the workplace and believes that women are not experiencing discrimination when seeking employment or advancing their careers. It publishes the *Women's Quarterly*, the quarterly *Ex Femina* newsletter, and special reports chronicling the economic progress of American women.

Industrial Relations Research Association (IRRA)
121 Labor and Industrial Relations
University of Illinois
504 E. Armory, MC-504, Champaign, IL 61820
(217) 333-0072 • fax (217) 265-5130
e-mail: irra@uiuc.edu • website: www.irra.uiuc.edu

IRRA is a nonpartisan membership organization that brings together those involved in academics, labor law, public policy, union administration, and economics to share ideas, issues, research, and practices in labor relations. It publishes the quarterly *IRRA Newsletter*, the magazine *Perspectives on Work*, and an annual research volume, past titles of which have included *Nonstandard Work Arrangement and the Changing Labor Market.*

Institute of Labor and Industrial Relations (ILIR)
Victor Vaughn Building, 1111 E. Catherine St.
Ann Arbor, MI 48109-2054
(734) 763-3116 • fax (734) 763-0913
e-mail: deh@umich.edu • website: www.ilir.umich.edu

ILIR conducts research on issues pertaining to labor unions and employment. Its Labor Studies Center offers education and training courses for the professional and personal development of workers in a rapidly changing employment environment. ILIR publishes numerous policy papers on poverty and unemployment, women and work, and labor unions.

International Center for Research on Women (ICRW)

1717 Massachusetts Ave. NW, Suite 302, Washington, DC 20036
(202) 797-0007 • fax (202) 797-0020
e-mail: info@icrw.org • website: www.icrw.org

ICRW is a nonprofit organization dedicated to promoting women's full participation in social and economic development. It conducts research and analysis aimed at improving the situation of poor women in developing countries. Its numerous publications cover the topics of woman-headed households, economics, and women in economic development.

International Labor Rights Fund (ILRF)

733 15th St. NW, Suite 920, Washington, DC 20005
(202) 347-4100 • fax: (202) 347-4885
e-mail: laborrights@igc.org • website: www.laborrights.org

The fund's research and education programs work to promote U.S. trade policies that ensure economic justice for workers in developing countries. It publishes numerous speeches, articles, and books on labor issues.

Labor Policy Association (LPA)

1015 15th St. NW, Suite 1200, Washington, DC 20005
(202) 789-8670 • fax (202) 789-0064
e-mail: info@lpa.org • website: www.lpa.org

LPA is a public policy association of human resource executives that provides analysis and opinion of current situations and emerging trends in labor and employment policy. It supports allowing more foreign professionals into the workforce and favors the flexibility of the contingent workforce, two of the issues covered in the numerous articles and reports that LPA publishes.

Labor Research Association (LRA)

330 W. 42nd St., 13th Floor, New York, NY 10036
(212) 714-1677 • fax (212) 714-1674
e-mail: info@laborresearch.org • website: www.laborresearch.org

This association supports labor unions by conducting research and compiling statistics on economic and political issues. It publishes the bimonthly *Economic Notes*, as well as reports on topics such as the low pay offered by many jobs, rising job insecurity, and the living wage movement.

National Alliance of Business (NAB)

1201 New York Ave. NW, Suite 700, Washington, DC 20005
(800) 787-2848 or (202) 289-2977 • fax (202) 289-2869
e-mail: info@nab.com • website: www.nab.com

The alliance works to shape social policies that will improve education, strengthen job training, and instill in workers the values essential to success in the modern workplace. It publishes the monthly newsletters *WorkAmerica* and *Workforce Economics*.

National Association of Workforce Boards (NAWB)

1201 New York Ave. NW, Suite 350, Washington, DC 20005
(202) 289-2950
e-mail: nawb@nawb.org • website: www.nawb.org

NAWB represents the interests of the nation's Workforce Investment Boards, which are local employer-led partnerships working to develop education, job training, and employment programs for the unemployed and economically disadvantaged. Its publications include the bimonthly newsletter, *Workforce Boards in Transition*.

National Center for Employee Ownership (NCEO)

1736 Franklin St., 8th Floor, Oakland, CA 94612-3445
(510) 208-1300 • fax (510) 272-9510
e-mail: nceo@nceo.org • website: www.nceo.org

This nonprofit information and education organization, whose membership includes companies, unions, and academics, promotes an increased awareness and understanding of employee-owned companies. It publishes numerous books on strategies for managing and working in an employee-owned company in addition to the bimonthly *Employee Ownership Report*.

National Committee on Pay Equity (NCPE)

3420 Hamilton St., Suite 200, Hyattsville, MD 20782
(301) 277-1033 • fax (301) 277-4451
e-mail: fairpay@aol.com • website: www.feminist.com/fairpay

NCPE is a national coalition of women's, labor, and civil rights organizations working to eliminate sex- and race-based wage discrimination and to achieve pay equity. Its publications include reports on the wage gap, the contingent workforce, minorities in the workplace, and the quarterly newsletter *Newsnotes*.

National Employment Law Project (NELP)
55 John St., 7th Floor, New York, NY 10038
(212) 285-3025 • fax (212) 285-3044
e-mail: nelp@nelp.org • website: www.nelp.org
NELP advocates on behalf of low-wage workers, the poor, the unemployed, and other groups facing barriers to employment by serving as a source of support and information for legal services attorneys, labor unions, and community groups. It publishes the biannual newsletter *NELP Update* and studies on the low-wage workforce, contingent workers, and discrimination in the workplace.

National Institute for Work and Learning (NIWL)
1825 Connecticut Ave. NW, Washington, DC 20009-5721
(202) 884-8186 • fax (202) 884-8422
e-mail: niwl@aed.org • website: www.niwl.org
The institute believes that the full development of human resources demands that education and work be treated as lifelong pursuits. It seeks to promote active collaboration between institutions of learning and work. Its projects include adult literacy centers and academic-business connections conferences. NIWL publishes several studies on the transition from school to work.

National Right to Work Committee (NRTWC)
8001 Braddock Rd., Suite 500, Springfield, VA 22160
(800) 325-7892 • fax (703) 321-7342
website: www.nrtwc.org
The committee is a labor reform group that conducts research and education programs to promote the belief that people should not be compelled to join labor unions in order to obtain jobs. It publishes the monthly *National Right to Work Newsletter* and legislative alerts relating to congressional action on labor policy.

The National School-to-Work Learning & Information Center
400 Virginia Ave. SW, Room 150, Washington, DC 20024
(800) 251-7236 or (202) 401-6222 • fax (202) 488-7395
e-mail: stw-lc@ed.gov • website: www.stw.ed.gov
Administered by the federal government, the center provides information on the progress of school-to-work programs around the country, including reports on how the programs can be strengthened through more parental and community support.

New Ways to Work
785 Market St., Suite 950, San Francisco, CA 94103
(415) 995-9860 • fax: (415) 995-9867
e-mail: info@nww.org • website: www.nww.org

Seeking to create a work world that better responds to the needs of workers, New Ways to Work promotes the concepts of flextime, job sharing, work sharing, and compressed workweeks. It publishes reports on creating flexible workplaces and managing contingent workers, and its projects include the School-to-Work Intermediary Project and Communities and Schools for Career Success.

9to5, National Association of Working Women
231 W. Wisconsin Ave., Suite 900, Milwaukee, WI 53203-2308
(414) 274-0925 • fax (414) 272-2870
website: www.9to5.org

The association is the leading membership organization for working women. It utilizes class-action lawsuits and public information campaigns to achieve change on issues such as discrimination against pregnant women, sexual harassment in the workplace, computer safety, and pay equity. In addition to reports on issues such as welfare-to-work and balancing work and families, it publishes the bimonthly *9to5 Newsline* newsletter.

Public Service Research Foundation (PSRF)
320-D Maple Ave. East, Vienna, VA 22180
(703) 242-3575 • fax (703) 242-3579
e-mail: info@psrf.org • website: www.psrf.org

This lobbying organization conducts research and public affairs programs on public sector employment, specifically on such issues as strikes, unions, and political spending. It opposes unionism in the public sector. The foundation publishes the journal *Government Union Review* and many articles critical of the unionization of the public sector.

Rockford Institute
928 N. Main St., Rockford, Illinois 61103
(815) 964-5053
e-mail: info@rockfordinstitute.org
website: www.rockfordinstitute.org

The institute advocates traditional roles for men and women and maintains that mothers who work or place their children in day care harm their children. It publishes the monthly magazine *Chronicles*.

U.S. Department of Health and Human Services

200 Independence Ave. SW, Washington, DC 20201
(877) 696-6775 or (202) 619-0257
e-mail: hhsmail@os.dhhs.gov • website: www.os.dhhs.gov

The secretary of health and human services advises the president on health, welfare, and income security plans, policies, and programs of the federal government. The department's many administrations and agencies can provide information and statistics on children and families, health care, or social security and welfare/workfare.

U.S. Department of Labor

200 Constitution Ave. NW, Room S-1032, Washington, DC 20210
(202) 693-4650
website: www.dol.gov

The Department of Labor administers a variety of federal labor laws guaranteeing workers' rights, a minimum wage, freedom from discrimination, and unemployment and workers' compensation insurance. Its public affairs office provides information on the department's policies and actions.

W.E. Upjohn Institute for Employment Research

300 S. Westnedge Ave., Kalamazoo, MI 49007-4686
(616) 343-5541 • fax (616) 343-3308
website: www.upjohninst.org

Funded by the nonprofit W.E. Upjohn Unemployment Trustee Corporation, this institute studies the causes and effects of unemployment, ways of insuring against unemployment, family employment issues, labor relations, and workforce equality. It publishes the quarterly newsletter *Employment Research* and books and papers on topics such as welfare reform's effects on reducing the real earnings of less-educated women.

Wider Opportunities for Women (WOW)

815 15th St. NW, Suite 916, Washington, DC 20005
(202) 638-3143 • fax (202) 638-4885
e-mail: info@WOWonline.org • website: www.wowonline.org

WOW works to expand employment opportunities for women by overcoming sex-stereotypic education and training, work segregation, and discrimination in employment practices and wages. It publishes the quarterly newsletter *Women at Work* and the biweekly *News Brief*, along with books and fact sheets.

Workers' Defense League (WDL)
275 Seventh Ave., New York, NY 10001
(212) 627-1931

This labor-oriented civil rights organization conducts educational campaigns to defend workers' rights and provides legal counseling to workers on employment-related problems. It publishes the quarterly *WDL News* as well as reports and pamphlets on workers' legal rights.

Work in America Institute
700 White Plains Rd., Scarsdale, NY 10583
(800) 787-0707 or (914) 472-9600 • fax (914) 472-9606
e-mail: info@workinamerica.org • website: www.workinamerica.org

The institute strives to improve U.S. productivity and the quality of working life through national research and a membership that brings together leaders from labor, management, government, and academia. Its publications include numerous case studies and reports on topics such as skills and career advancement, employment security, and continuing education.

Bibliography of Books

Stanley Aronowitz — *From the Ashes of the Old: American Labor and America's Future.* New York: Basic Books, 2000.

Steve Babson — *The Unfinished Struggle: Turning Points in American Labor, 1877–Present.* Lanham, MD: Rowman & Littlefield, 1999.

Kathleen Barker and Kathleen Christensen — *Contingent Work: American Employment Relations in Transition.* Ithaca, NY: ILR Press, 1998.

Barbara R. Bergmann — *In Defense of Affirmative Action.* New York: BasicBooks, 1996.

Sandra E. Black and Lisa M. Lynch — *What's Driving the New Economy: The Benefits of Workplace Innovation.* Cambridge, MA: National Bureau of Economic Research, 2000.

Francine D. Blau and Lawrence M. Kahn — *Gender Differences in Pay.* Cambridge, MA: National Bureau of Economic Research, 2000.

David Boaz — *Libertarianism: A Primer.* New York: Free Press, 1997.

Vernon M. Briggs Jr. — *Immigration and American Unionism.* Ithaca, NY: ILR Press, 2001.

Harry Browne — *Why Government Doesn't Work.* New York: St. Martin's Press, 1995.

Christina Cregan — *Young People in the Workplace: Job, Union, and Mobility Patterns.* New York: Mansell, 1999.

Colin Crouch, David Finegold, and Mari Sako — *Are Skills the Answer?* New York: Oxford University Press, 1999.

Michael R. Darby, ed. — *Reducing Poverty in America: Views and Approaches.* Thousand Oaks, CA: Sage Publications, 1996.

Taylor E. Dark — *The Unions and the Democrats: An Enduring Alliance.* Ithaca, NY: ILR Press, 1999.

Dana Dunn, ed. — *Workplace/Women's Place: An Anthology.* Los Angeles: Roxbury Publishing, 1997.

J. Michael Farr — *America's Fastest Growing Jobs: Details on the Best Jobs at All Levels of Training and Education.* Indianapolis: Jist Works, 1999.

Robert C. Feenstra, ed. — *The Impact of International Trade on Wages.* Chicago: University of Chicago Press, 2000.

Marianne A. Ferber and Julie A. Nelson, eds. — *Women at the End of the Millennium: What We Know, What We Need to Know.* Stamford, CT: JAI Press, 1999.

Lawrence B. Glickman | *A Living Wage: American Workers and the Making of Consumer Society*. Ithaca, NY: Cornell University Press, 1997.

Morley Gunderson | *Comparable Worth and Gender Discrimination: An International Perspective*. Geneva: International Labour Office, 1994.

Edmund Heery and John Salmon | *The Insecure Workforce*. New York: Routledge, 2000.

Sharlene Hesse-Biber and Gregg Lee Carter | *Working Women in America: Split Dreams*. New York: Oxford University Press, 2000.

Randy Hodson, ed. | *Marginal Employment*. Stamford, CT: JAI Press, 2000.

Harry J. Holzer and David Neumark | *Are Affirmative Action Hires Less Qualified? Evidence from Employer-Employee Data on New Hires*. Cambridge, MA: National Bureau of Economic Research, 1996.

Harry J. Holzer and Michael A. Stoll | *Employers and Welfare Recipients: The Effects of Welfare Reform in the Workplace*. San Francisco: Public Policy Institute of California, 2001.

Harry C. Katz and Owen Darbishire | *Converging Divergences: Worldwide Changes in Employment Systems*. Ithaca, NY: Cornell University Press, 2000.

Suzanne Knell | *Learning to Earn: Issues Raised by Welfare Reform for Adult Education, Training, and Work*. Washington, DC: National Institute for Literacy, 1998.

Marvin H. Kosters, ed. | *The Effects of Minimum Wage on Employment*. Washington, DC: AEI Press, 1996.

Staughton Lynd and Alice Lynd, eds. | *The New Rank and File*. Ithaca, NY: ILR Press, 2000.

Karen J. Maschke, ed. | *The Employment Context*. New York: Garland, 1997.

Patrick L. Mason | *African Americans, Labor, and Society: Organizing for a New Agenda*. Detroit: Wayne State University Press, 2001.

Ruth Milkman, ed. | *Organizing Immigrants: The Challenge for Unions in Contemporary California*. Ithaca, NY: ILR Press, 2000.

Garrett Murphy and Alice Johnson | *What Works: Integrating Basic Skills Training into Welfare-to-Work*. Washington, DC: National Institute for Literacy, 1998.

Bruce Nelson | *Divided We Stand: American Workers and the Struggle for Black Equality*. Princeton, NJ: Princeton University Press, 2001.

Robert L. Nelson and William P. Bridges

Legalizing Gender Inequality: Courts, Markets, and Unequal Pay for Women in America. New York: Cambridge University Press, 1999.

David Neumark and Scott Adams

Do Living Wage Ordinances Reduce Urban Poverty? Cambridge, MA: National Bureau of Economic Research, 2000.

Paul Osterman

The American Labor Market: How It Has Changed and What to Do About It. Princton, NJ: Princeton University Press, 1999.

Robert Pollin and Stephanie Luce

The Living Wage: Building a Fair Economy. New York: New Press, 1998.

Frederic L. Pryor and David L. Schaffer

Who's Not Working and Why: Employment, Cognitive Skills, Wages, and the Changing U.S. Labor Market. New York: Cambridge University Press, 1999.

David S. Salkever and Alan Sorkin

The Economics of Disability. Stamford, CT: JAI Press, 2000.

Kenneth F. Scheve and Matthew J. Slaughter

Globalization and the Perceptions of American Workers. Washington, DC: Institute for International Economics, 2001.

Elaine Sorensen

Comparable Worth: Is It a Worthy Policy? Princeton, NJ: Princeton University Press, 1994.

Fredelle Zaiman Spiegel

Women's Wages, Women's Worth: Politics, Religion, Equity. New York: Continuum, 1994.

Gail E. Thomas

Race and Ethnicity in America: Meeting the Challenge in the 21st Century. Washington, DC: Taylor & Francis, 1995.

Ray M. Tillman and Michael S. Cummings, eds.

The Transformation of U.S. Unions: Voices, Visions, and Strategies from the Grassroots. Boulder, CO: Lynne Rienner Publishers, 1999.

Jerold Waltman

The Politics of the Minimum Wage. Urbana: University of Illinois Press, 2000.

Jane Wheelock and John Vail

Work and Idleness: The Political Economy of Full Employment. Boston: Kluwer Academic Publishers, 1998.

Joan Williams

Unbending Gender. New York: Oxford University Press, 2000.

Index